Halloween
Costumes · Parties · Activities · Recipes

Susie Johns

MQP

Published by MQ Publications Limited
12 The Ivories, 6–8 Northampton Street
London N1 2HY
Tel: 020 7359 2244
Fax: 020 7359 1616
www.mqpublications.com

ISBN: 1-84072-719-5

1 3 5 7 9 0 8 6 4 2

Printed and bound in China

Contents

Introduction **6**

Costumes and Disguises **8**

Decorations and Party Stuff **104**

Food **168**

Games and Activities **216**

Halloween for Grown-ups **312**

History and Legend **360**

Customs and Superstitions **402**

Introduction

When I was a child, I remember a Halloween party at the local church hall. My mother dressed me up as a witch. She pummeled the black hat from my traditional Welsh costume to make it more pointed in shape. I had to hold my face in a ghastly grimace while she etched lines and wrinkles with an eyebrow pencil. By the time she had finished, I looked suitably hag-like.

Halloween celebrates everything to do with this fearsome festival. Choose from a wide variety of traditional and inventive games that will help to make Halloween a scream. There are also ideas for decorating your home—plus creative and crazy suggestions for all kinds of costumes and disguises.

Read on to discover the fascinating history of Halloween and some of the weird and wonderful customs that have been practiced, and still prevail today in some parts of the world.

Every Halloween, my kids and I put on costumes— I still dress up as a witch—and decorate our own house. We go trick-or-treating, visit neighbors, and then return home for hot punch and some edible homemade treats. Take a look at the chapter on food, where you will find plenty of delicious delicacies to choose from.

However you decide to celebrate, I hope you will find some inspirational ideas in the pages of this book. Have a *horrrrible* Halloween!

Costumes
and
Disguises

SPIDER. Wear a black leotard and tights. Stuff two pairs of black tights with crumpled black tissue paper or shredded fabric. Fasten a belt around your waist, trapping the stuffed tights at the back, to make four legs (your arms and legs make the other four). Add a black knit hat with black pipe cleaners for antennae.

MUMMY. Cover your face with white face paint and wrap your whole body, arms, legs, and head with bandages or strips of white muslin or cheesecloth.

What kind of tie does a ghost wear to a formal party?
—A boo tie.

SKELETON. Decorate a black leotard and tights with white tape or ribbon, glued or stitched in place to denote ribs and arms and leg bones.

CRASH TEST DUMMY. Decorate a plain track suit with markings in white tape. Add a seat belt made from webbing and an old buckle.

DRUID. A hooded brown bathrobe, several sizes too big, makes a good basic garment. It's also useful for a mad monk. If you can't find a bathrobe like this, improvise with a long piece of brown fabric, draping it over your head and, using safety pins on the inside, pinning it shut along the sides. Add a belt and sandals.

DEVIL. Start with a red leotard and tights and add a long tail and horns, homemade or from a joke shop.

DRACULA. Wear a black dinner suit, wing-collared shirt, and bow tie. Slick your hair back with gel and make your face pale with white makeup. Add black eyeliner and a little black face paint to accentuate or create a widow's peak. Don't forget to add plastic fangs and a black cloak.

BRIDE OF DRACULA. Wear a slinky, long dress, and long gloves. Wear your hair loose, if it is long, or purchase a long black wig. White makeup, red lipstick, and fangs will complete the look.

ANGEL. You can make a long white robe from an old white sheet with a hole cut in it for your head. Slip it on and tie a white or gold belt or cord around your waist. Add angel's wings—buy some or make them at home from white or gold-painted cardboard—and a halo made from a wire coat hanger bent into shape and wrapped with gold tinsel or aluminum foil.

FAIRY. Put on your prettiest tutu with tights and, of course, a pair of wings. If you want to be the queen of the fairies, add a sparkling crown.

FLOWER FAIRY. Start with a basic costume of a ballet dress or a sleeveless camisole and a full skirt. Add wings and pin leaves and fabric flowers all over your clothes. Wear a flower garland in your hair.

BAD FAIRY. Start with a black or purple tutu and matching tights, which could be full of holes, and clumpy boots instead of ballet slippers. Long black gloves look good, too. Mess up your hair and go mad with your makeup—black eyeliner and black or purple lipstick, for example. And don't forget your wings—make them black, not white or gold.

To make a net skirt that's suitable for a fairy or ballerina, you will need about 2 yards (1.8 m) of netting and $1\frac{1}{2}$ yards (1.4 m) of wide ribbon. Fold the net in half lengthways and sew through the double fold of fabric, about $\frac{1}{2}$ inch (1 cm) from the fold, with a running stitch. Pull up the thread to gather the fabric until the gathered edge is the same as your waist measurement. Stitch the ribbon over the gathered edge, leaving about 10 inches (25 cm) to spare on both ends. Wrap the skirt around yourself and tie the ribbon ends. Netting is inexpensive and available in a wide range of colors.

FAIRY WINGS. Bend two wire coat hangers into wing shapes, taping the sharp ends together to form the center of the pair of wings. Cut the legs off a pair of tights and stretch one over each wire wing frame. Tape the cut edges of the tights together at the point where the wings are joined. Cut two 14-inch (35 cm) pieces of elastic and attach them to the center of the wings so they make loops to slip over your shoulders. Decorate the wings with dimensional fabric paints, squeezing patterns straight from the tube and let them dry overnight before bending into shape.

For a fairy wand, cut two star shapes from thick cardboard. Place the end of a stick on one, cover the star and the stick with glue, and press the other star shape over the first to glue them together. When the star has dried, paint it and the stick, gluing on some jewels or glitter if you like. Tie ribbon streamers around the top of the stick.

GYPSY. Make sure you have a big spotted scarf tied around your head, and big hoop earrings. Cover your face and hands with tan makeup. Girls can wear full skirts, a puff-sleeved blouse, and a shawl, with lots of rings and bracelets. Boys can wear a loose white shirt and tight pants tucked into boots, as well as a vest and colorful sash.

CAN-CAN DANCER. Wear a leotard or a tight bodice with fishnet tights. Add several petticoats and a colorful gathered skirt. Add ballet slippers with ribbon bows attached. Wear a wide hairband and stick in an ostrich feather or two.

SKIN DIVER. Wear a wet suit, if you have one, or a gray track suit. Add swimming goggles, flippers, and a snorkel. You could even carry a bucket filled with plastic fish.

MEDIEVAL PEASANT.
Cut off canvas or khaki
pants below the knee
and wear them with a
loose linen or cotton
shirt with a wide strip
of burlap draped
around your shoulders
to form a rough tunic.
Make a belt from a
narrower fabric strip
or piece of rope.

MEDIEVAL MAIDEN. Wrap some burlap around your waist and tie it in place with a strip of fabric to make a skirt. Take a rectangle of similar fabric, cut a hole in the center and put your head through it to make a tunic. Drape yet more fabric around your head for a hood.

JACK-IN-THE-BOX. Stick your legs through a big cardboard box and hold it up with suspenders. If you can find enough old slinky toys, cover your arms with them. If not, wear a shirt with long sleeves. Put on a stocking cap and decorate the box or paint it.

SHERIFF. Wear trousers tucked into some cowboy boots and a shirt, vest, and shoelace tie. A cowboy hat, a star-shaped badge, and a gun belt complete the outfit.

OUTLAW. A checked shirt, vest, jeans, cowboy boots, and hat will turn you into a cowboy. Add a scarf folded into a triangle and worn as a mask, a droopy mustache, and a scar to look like a wanted man.

NATIVE INDIAN. Loose pants and a tunic top are a good start for this costume, but you could just add fringe and beads to a plain T-shirt. Search in thrift stores or yard sales for a pair of moccasins or soft boots and lots of bead necklaces. Add a feathered headdress.

To make a simple feather headband, cut a strip of corrugated cardboard long enough to go around your head and about 2 inches (5 cm) wide. Join the two ends. Glue paper cutouts onto the band for decorations and push feathers into the ridges in the corrugations. Use a dab of glue to hold them in place.

For a more elaborate feathered headdress, start with a band of corrugated cardboard, and stick a semicircle of cardboard onto the front of it. Staple long feathers, evenly spaced, on the inside of the top, curved edge. Cover the staple ends that show on the front of the cardboard with glued-on paper or decorations. Braid strands of colored string or ribbons together, tie beads and small feathers to the ends of the braids, and glue them to the headband as if they were real braids.

EARLY AMERICAN SETTLER. Conjure up old colonial times with a powdered wig and a fancy dress for a girl or a vest of richly embroidered fabric and long shorts for a boy, with white tights and buckled shoes for both.

1950s. Girls can wear a poodle skirt or capri pants with a skinny top, bobby socks and sneakers, and put their hair in a ponytail. Boys could be a rock 'n' roll star in drainpipe pants and a jeans jacket, or a suit with a shirt and a thin tie!

MONSTER. Wear an oversized track suit and stuff it with crumpled newspapers to create a misshapen silhouette. Fake rubber feet would be a nice touch, otherwise, cut gruesome toenails from craft foam and glue them onto rubber boots.

CLOWN. Use clothes that are too large— a striped T-shirt, checked pants, a vest or jacket—then add colorful socks, suspenders to hold up the pants, and boots. You could add some large, colorful pom-poms to the front of the shirt and wear a hat on top of a novelty wig.

SCARECROW. Wear a large checked shirt, patched jeans held up with a rope belt, and more rope tied around the cuffs of the jeans and sleeves. Stuff the shirt and jeans with crumpled paper and have a little bit of straw poking out. Add a straw hat—maybe with a little bird attached.

FARMER. Wear loose cotton or corduroy pants, tucked into rubber boots. Wear a checked shirt, a neckerchief, and a battered straw hat. Carry a sturdy walking stick and a toy lamb under your arm.

RAG DOLL. Sew fabric patches on to a track suit or all-in-one sleep suit. For a raggedy wig, stitch strips of fabric to a knit hat. Rouge your cheeks, put on red lipstick, and add some freckles with a brown eye pencil.

RAGAMUFFIN. Choose old clothes that you can cut up. Cut the bottoms off a pair of pants two sizes too large and fray the edges. Wear them with an old belt to pull them in around your waist, and a shirt with rolled-up sleeves. Add a cloth cap worn at a jaunty angle and smudge brown makeup on your cheeks and nose. Make a bundle from a stick and a red spotted handkerchief.

FRANKENSTEIN'S MONSTER.
The main feature is the head—and
a purchased mask is a good option.
Wear a suit, with pants that are too
short and a shirt padded with
newspapers or spare clothing and
ripped in places to suggest that
it's too small.

DR. FRANKENSTEIN OR NUTTY PROFESSOR. Wear a lab coat over your normal clothes and a pair of wire-rimmed glasses. You could backcomb your hair and add a few gray smudges to your face—as if you have been experimenting in the lab with something explosive.

SORCERER. Make a simple cloak from a rectangle of satin gathered at the neck edge. Sew ribbon onto it so you can tie it around your neck. Underneath, you could wear black pants and a plain black sweater. A cone-shaped hat may be covered in fabric to match the cloak, and a wand completes the outfit.

Use tubes of dimensional paint in white or silver to decorate plain black clothing or black fabric that you'll use as a cloak.

WEREWOLF. A brown track suit would make a good start for this costume, and so would a brown jacket and pants in a slightly hairy tweed. Backcomb your hair and paint on a widow's peak using face paints. You could also try sticking short lengths of false hair on your face, with a special adhesive gum that's available from most stores that sell or rent costumes. And don't forget a set of plastic fangs!

ALIEN. Dress up as a little green creature, in green tights and T-shirt, with antennae formed out of green drinking straws or pipe cleaners sticking out of your head. Attach the antennae to a hairband to keep them in the right spot.

GHOST. Find an old white sheet and cut out holes for the eyes. Drape it over your head and body. Easy!

DRESSED-UP GHOST. On your plain white sheet, paint eyelashes around the eye holes and patches of red on the cheeks. You could add a necklace, a boa, or a fancy hat.

What do baby ghosts wear on their feet?
—Boo-ties!

AMERICAN TOURIST. If you are a boy, you could wear a Hawaiian shirt or a summer T-shirt with Bermuda shorts and a baseball cap. Girls could wear a short-sleeved shirt with a cardigan on top, a full skirt with a belt, and short socks with gym shoes. Have a camera slung around your neck, sunglasses, and maps sticking out of pockets.

HIPPY. Wear tie-dyed clothing, a long wig, flared pants or a long skirt, sandals, a headband, a fringed vest or a shaggy afghan coat, and pink sunglasses—plus lots and lots of beads and flowers in your hair.

OLD MAN. Wear a dark suit with a vest or tweed pants with a shirt and cardigan. You could add a golf cap or a derby hat and carry a walking stick. Try graying your hair, using a commercial temporary color if you are blonde or dusting it with talcum powder or flour if you're dark.

OLD WOMAN. Wear a skirt or dress that falls just below the knee with a cardigan, white socks, and shoes with small heels. A pearl necklace and earrings and a curly gray wig help to create a believable character—not to mention a walking stick and old-fashioned handbag.

NERD. Wear pants that are too short with white socks and lace-up shoes and a white, short-sleeved shirt with lots of pens in the breast pocket. Put on wire-rimmed or tortoiseshell-framed glasses, repaired with a piece of surgical tape. Paint some red spots on your face and put lots of grease in your hair.

MOVIE STAR. Girls can wear a sparkly or shimmery dress with a fancy handbag, high-heeled shoes, a wrap or shawl, and some jewelry. Boys look good in a black suit, white shirt, and bow tie. Search local thrift stores or yard sales for cheap secondhand suits and other glamorous items!

ROCK STAR. Tight jeans and denim jackets with skimpy vests are a good start. Girls can also wear mini-dresses, sparkly tights, and high-heeled shoes. Make sure your hair and makeup look as glamorous as your clothes.

PUNK. Slash an old T-shirt and wear it with plain or tartan pants and lots of belts and chains. Make your face a few shades paler than usual with makeup and spike up your hair with stiff gel.

Why do mummies have trouble keeping friends?

—They're too wrapped up in themselves.

GOTH. Dress all in black. Long skirts, layered on top of each other with the top layers torn and ragged, fishnet tights, gloves, and lots of lace makes a great look for girls. Boys might like to add a leather jacket and a top hat. Once again, pale faces and untidy hair are part of the costume.

MISS HAVISHAM. For this creepy character from Dickens' *Great Expectations*, use an old wedding dress or a fancy white nightie from a thrift store or yard sale and make sure it is ripped and tattered. Add long white gloves, a tiara, diamond or pearl jewelry, and a piece of white netting for a veil.

CLEOPATRA. Make a simple dress from a large rectangle of fabric—metallic gold looks great—with a hole cut in the center. Put your head through the hole, wrap the fabric around you, and fasten it with a belt. Wear a black wig, gold hairband, sandals, and lots of jewelry—necklaces and a snake bracelet. You can also make a wide collar from gold paper or fabric decorated with stick-on jewels. Boys could adapt this costume to dress as King Tutankhamun.

QUASIMODO. Wear an old coat several sizes too large and stuff a cushion or a large wad of crumpled newspapers up the back and around the shoulders to create a hump. Wear cut-off, ragged pants and a messy wig.

PIRATE. Wear wide-legged pants and a striped top, perhaps with a vest. Tie a spotted bandana around your head, wear an eye patch, and carry a sword or an empty rum bottle. A stuffed parrot is optional.

To make a pirate shirt, take a plain or striped T-shirt and cut off the neckband and shorten the sleeves, if necessary. Cut a skull and crossbones from white fabric and stick this to the front of the shirt, using fabric glue.

PIRATE CAPTAIN. A white shirt, preferably with frills, worn with knee britches and boots creates a great costume. Add a jacket with tails and brass buttons, a silk sash or wide leather buckled belt, and a three-cornered hat with an ostrich feather for an added flourish.

AL CAPONE. A classic gangster costume requires a pinstripe suit, black shirt, white tie, hat, and a toy machine gun—don't forget a threatening facial expression!

BONNIE AND CLYDE. He can dress as a classic gangster; she should wear a suit and skirt, maybe in a pinstripe fabric to match her accomplice, with a long, straight wig and a beret.

ELVIS. Buy a spandex jumpsuit from a thrift store and decorate it by sticking on fake jewels. Add a big collar cut from card and covered with shiny fabric. Then gel your hair into an impressive curl at the front.

ISLAND GIRL. Make a hula skirt from strips of crepe paper attached to a length of wide elastic long enough to go around your waist. Wear it with a bikini or a skimpy top, garlands of fabric flowers, and beads around your wrists and ankles. (In cold weather, you would be wise to wear a skin-colored leotard and tights with this costume!)

To make a great hula-hula garland, cut strips from colorful plastic shopping bags and colored tissue paper. Each strip should measure about 5 inches (12.5 cm) wide and between 30 to 40 inches (80 to 100 cm) long. For each garland, sandwich two or three strips of tissue paper between two strips of plastic. Using a needle and thread, stitch up the center, through all layers, and then join the two ends. Make a fringe by snipping it on both sides of the center stitching and then crumple and ruffle the garland in your hands.

**What do you get when you cross
Bambi with a ghost?
—Bamboo.**

ARTIST. Use old clothes—a loose shirt
and pants—and spatter them with
paint. Wear a beret or a flamboyant hat
and a colorful scarf tied around your
neck. Carry a palette and have a pencil
or paintbrush tucked behind one ear.

SUPERHERO. Wear colored tights with underwear over the top and a tight T-shirt with a symbol painted on with fabric paint or cut out of colored fabric and pinned in place. Stretch a knit cap over your hair and wear a mask to hide your eyes. Add a cape as a final flourish.

ACTION MAN. Wear battle fatigues, sturdy boots, and a beret. Sling climbing ropes across your chest and carry a backpack. You could even smudge camouflage paint on your face.

CAVEMAN. Start with an old T-shirt or dress in plain beige or brown, or in an animal print. Cut off its sleeves and snip the armholes and hem to create a jagged edge. Keep any long strips you cut off to tie around wrists, ankles, and head. Wear sandals, mess up your hair, and carry a big wooden club (a stick will do).

KING. Start with long socks and britches made from cut-off pants. Wear a fancy shirt on top and a cloak, preferably trimmed with fur. A crown is an absolute must—you could add a long wig as well—and plenty of gold chains and other fancy jewelry.

PRINCESS. Wear a long dress of shiny or sparkly material and a cloak. Add a crown, of course, and plenty of jewelry.

Where do fashionable ghosts
go shopping?
—In boo-tiques.

**COURT JESTER. If you can, take a
red track suit and a yellow one, and
cut both their tops and pants up the
middle. Then stitch a yellow half to a
red half. Do the same with a red and
yellow hat. You will now have two
costumes, so you and a friend could
dress up as a pair of jesters. A nice
touch is to sew on some bells so
that you jingle when you walk.**

ELF. Wear green all over, whether it is a leotard and tights or a track suit. Make pointed shoes to slip over your normal shoes from felt. Even if you can't sew, you could cut out felt shapes and glue them together. Use a felt tie to hold them around your ankles. While you're at it, make a pointed green felt hat with a bell on the end. Another nice touch is to cut out a ring of yellow felt, with a bold, zigzag edge, to slip around your neck as a collar. If you are really getting carried away with scissors, felt, and glue, you could also make yourself a pair of matching zigzag-edged cuffs.

Dress like Morticia, from the Addams Family, in a long, slinky dress. A red dress with a black lace dress over the top looks great. Wear a long black wig and false fingernails and make your face very white, with red lips and plenty of heavy black eyeliner.

RAP STAR. Wear a shiny track suit, with the jacket unzipped, over a slinky T-shirt or vest. Add a pair of shades and lots of gold chains and other large jewelry—and be sure to adopt a bad attitude!

SNOWMAN. Wear an oversized white track suit, stuffed with crumpled paper, and white shoes and socks. Add a hat, mittens, scarf, and black pom-poms for buttons.

SANTA. A red track suit is a great start. Add a wide belt, black boots, and plenty of white fur trim—plus a white beard, of course.

ROBIN HOOD. Dress in green tights and make a tabard from a rectangle of green fabric with a hole cut for your head. Wear a leather belt around your waist and carry a bow and a quiver full of arrows. You can make a hat quite easily from two triangles of green felt with a feather added.

BRAVEHEART. Think of Mel Gibson in the film. Wear a linen shirt and make your own ancient kilt by wrapping a long length of tartan fabric around your waist and over one shoulder. Hold everything in place with a leather belt around your waist. Mess up your hair and paint half your face blue. A wooden sword is a good accessory.

SKIER. Wear ski clothing—a snow suit, wool hat, scarf, sunglasses, and gloves—and wrap your "broken" leg in a bandage.

BAT. You will need an old black umbrella. Discard the handle and cut the umbrella in half. Wear a black track suit, or leotard and tights, and attach the umbrella pieces to the sleeves. A black knit hat with pointed ears cut from black cardboard or craft foam and glued in place looks effective.

ZORRO. Dress all in black. You will need tight black pants, tucked into black boots, a black satin shirt, black hat, cape, and mask. Sling a leather belt diagonally across your body and carry a sword.

SKUNK. Wear a black leotard and tights or a black track suit and glue a long strip of white fabric down your back.

TURTLE. Dress in a green track suit and make a shell from a large piece of cardboard, cut to shape and decorated with paints or marker pens. Pierce holes in the shell and add loops of elastic which will slip over your shoulders to hold it in place.

HARRY POTTER. Wear school uniform, complete with tie, but add a robe and a pair of wire-rimmed spectacles, and carry a magic wand and a book of spells.

How do you mend a broken jack-o'-lantern?
—With a pumpkin patch.

Dress up as a character from a scary movie!
Use books, movie posters, videos, or the
internet for ideas.

BUNNY RABBIT. Start with a brown, gray
or white track suit, or a leotard and tights.
Pin a white powder puff or large pom-
pom to the back and make a pair of ears
from paper attached to a headband.

**PUPPY DOG. Wear a brown, black, or white
track suit or a leotard and tights, decorated
with glued-on spots cut from a contrasting
colored paper or fabric. Make floppy ears from
cardboard or fabric and attach these to a
headband, and pin on a tail made from fabric
or rope. You could also wear a dog collar.**

PUSSY CAT. This is a variation on the rabbit and the dog—just make pointed ears and a longer tail. You could also wear a collar or a floppy ribbon bow pinned to the neck band of your costume.

LADYBUG. Dress in a black track suit or leotard and tights and black shoes. Cut a large oval from cardboard and paint it red with black spots. Pierce holes in the cardboard and add loops of elastic which will slip over your shoulders to hold it in place. Make antennae from pipe cleaners with black pom-poms on the ends, attached to a headband.

Did you hear about the little boy who was upset when he won first prize for the best costume at the Halloween party?
—He'd only come to pick up his sister!

LAUNDRY BASKET. Cut a hole in the base of a cheap plastic laundry basket and slip it over your head so the basket sits on your hips. Fill it with laundry and an empty packet of detergent, and pin a few items—socks and T-shirts—to your own clothing.

CARBONATED DRINK. Make a round tube shape from corrugated cardboard and cut holes for arms. Paint it to look like a can of your favorite soft drink. Stick plastic straws in your hair.

PLAYING CARD. Cut two large rectangles of cardboard and paint them with a playing card design—a Queen, King, or Jack if you are good at painting, or an ace or number card if you want to keep it simple, on one side, and a design on the other. Join the tops of the cardboard pieces by attaching lengths of ribbon or tape to form shoulder straps, and wear your cards like a sandwich board.

TV NEWSREADER. Cut a hole in the base of a cardboard box that's large enough to fit over your head. Cut a large hole for the screen from the front panel. Stick on dials and add an aerial to the top. Dress smartly and carry a pile of papers with you.

REFRIGERATOR. Cut a hole in a large cardboard box, paint the box white, and glue on a cardboard handle. Use a silver marker pen to write the manufacturer's name on the front. Glue an assortment of fridge magnets and a shopping list to the front.

GIFT BOX. Cut a hole in a large cardboard box that's big enough to go over your body. Cover the box with wrapping paper and tie a big bow around it. Cut a big gift tag from cardboard and attach it with string. Suspend the box on your shoulders and cut armholes so you can use your hands!

DINNER TABLE. Cut a head hole in a large cardboard box and drape it with white fabric or an old tablecloth that you can cut into. Cut a hole in the cloth for your head and glue plastic tableware on your table top—plates, cutlery, glasses, even a plastic candelabra if you can find one.

DICE. Paint a large cardboard box white or a plain color of your choice. The side where you cut the head hole can represent number one. Cut paper circles and stick them in place on the other sides, for numbers two to six.

AIRPLANE. A cardboard box can easily have cardboard wings, a propeller, and a tail. Cut a hole in the box large enough so it will slip right over your shoulders and sit comfortably around your waist. You may need to add shoulder straps to keep it in place.

If you don't want to wear a "silly" costume, you could always decorate your regular clothes. Cut Halloween designs from fabric and pin them to your sweatshirt or the back of your jacket. For a more permanent decoration, glue on fabric cut-outs with fabric glue, or cut designs from iron-on patching material.

Customize a Halloween T-shirt. Try tie-dyeing! If you are dyeing a new T-shirt, you will need to wash it first to be certain that the dye can penetrate the fabric. For a swirled effect, lay the T-shirt flat, pinch the center with your finger and thumb, and twist the fabric into a spiral. Secure the twisted bundle with rubber bands, placing them at three locations on the spiral. Make up three colors of dye according to the packet instructions. Green, orange, and black are the classic Halloween colors. Protect your work surface with plastic bags and your hands with rubber gloves. Use a paintbrush to apply dye to the T-shirt, painting each section a different color. Make sure the fabric is well saturated with dye. Place the T-shirt in a plastic bag, seal the bag, and leave it overnight. When you remove it, rinse the shirt in cold water until the water runs clear, and then remove the rubber bands. Wash your T-shirt in hot, soapy water, rinse, and dry. When buying dyes, ask for advice at the store. You will need cold water dyes that are suitable for cotton fabrics and are permanent so that they won't wash out.

You could dye
other items of
clothing, too.
If you don't have
enough black
clothes for your
costume, try
dyeing old cotton
pants, socks,
or track suits.

Wheelchair users can adapt any of the ideas in this chapter, or try one of the following, which incorporate the chair as part of the costume.

KING OR QUEEN. Convert your wheelchair into a throne by wrapping the back and arm rests with gold or silver aluminum foil or wrapping paper. Decorate it with fake gemstones, old jewelry or tinsel. Dress in a red or purple cape, preferably with a fur collar, and a crown. Carry an orb and scepter.

A boy went to a Halloween party wrapped in a sheet.
"Are you a ghost?" asked his friends.
—"No," he said, "I've just got out of bed."

**VENTRILOQUIST. Borrow a ventriloquist's dummy
and wear a dinner suit or dress to match the doll.**

GIFT. Find a box that will fit over you
and the chair. Cut a hole in the top for
your head and one on each side for
your arms, then decorate it with
wrapping paper and ribbons. Decorate
a smaller box in a similar way to wear
as a hat or tie a huge ribbon bow in
your hair, adding a giant gift tag.

JACK-IN-THE-BOX. Once again, find a big box and cut holes for your head and arms. Cover the box in brightly colored paper and wear clown makeup and a funny hat.

CAR OR TRUCK. Use a large box with holes cut in it. Stick a smaller box on the front, for the hood, and another at the back for a trunk. Paint it a bright color, adding windows and other details such as door handles. Cover jar lids with metallic paper and glue them to the front for headlights.

FANTASY FACES. Face paints are for kids of all ages and you can use them to create some stunning effects. By applying paint with a damp sponge, you can create subtle blends of color or you can use a fine, soft paintbrush to paint lines, dots, and other details. Before you start on your face—or someone else's—experiment on the back of your hand.

WICKED WITCH. With a sponge, cover your whole face with green face paint and add an outline of purple around the jawline, using the sponge to blend the colors together where they join. With a brush, paint a red line under each eye and paint black eyebrows and wrinkles around your eyes, nose, and mouth and creases on your lips. Use the tip of the brush to paint red spots on your chin and forehead and outline these in black.

How do witches keep their hair in place?
—With scare spray.

Why does a witch fly on a broom?
—Because a vacuum cleaner would be too heavy.

What does a cool witch ride instead of
a motorcycle?
—A brrr-oomstick!

What has a black hat, flies on a broomstick, and can't see anything?
—A witch with her eyes closed.

For a paler witch or wizard, cover your face in white face paint. With black face paint and a brush, draw in eyebrows above your natural brow line and outline your eyes, sweeping up the lines at the outer corners. Paint green face paint on your eyelids and mouth. You could add a touch of glitter to your face and hair.

OLD HAG. Sponge gray or yellowish-gray face paint all over your face, including your mouth. Using brown face paint and a medium-fine brush, darken your eyelids and paint lines under your eyes, from the inner corners out towards the cheeks. Paint more lines radiating from the outer corners of the eyes, like crows' feet, and from the nose to the outer corners of your mouth. For the mouth itself, paint a thin line right across, where your lips meet, then paint lines radiating outwards to the edges of your natural lipline. All these lines should make you look old and wrinkled, and mean and nasty. With the same brush and some black face paint, go over some of the lines on your mouth and then paint in bushy black eyebrows.

For a blotchy skin tone, that is also good for witches, cover your face with dots of green and white face paint and blend them together with your fingertips.

JACK-O'-LANTERN. Paint your whole face orange. With black face paint and a brush, paint triangles around your eyes and nose and add a really big, zigzag mouth.

SPIDERWOMAN. Cover your face with white face paint, applied with a sponge to create an even layer and paint spiders crawling up your cheeks with black face paint and a fine brush.

SKELETON. Cover your face with white face paint, then paint in hollow eyes, a nose, a mouth, and cheeks with black face paint.

DEVIL. You will need red face paint—and plenty of it. Look for it at a costume or novelty store. Cover your face, neck, and ears—in fact, all the exposed areas of your skin. For a wicked leer, paint arched eyebrows in black above your natural eyebrow line.

LITTLE DEVIL HAND PUPPET. Use a sponge to apply red face paint all over the palm and the back of your hand, your wrist, and your thumb. Then paint the forefinger and little finger white, and the middle two fingers black. Also paint the tip of your thumb and base of your little finger black. Paint a devil's face and beard on your palm, blocking in the eyes and teeth with white face paint then outlining them in black. Tie a red scarf or fabric remnant around your wrist.

Angels, fairies, and princesses can stay au naturel or you can add touches of lip gloss and glitter.

What happened to the girl who went to a Halloween party dressed as a mouse?
—The cat ate her!

Look out for face putty or wax, available from theatrical suppliers and some novelty stores. It can be molded and stuck in place to form warts, lumps, scars, and other scary effects!

Peasants, tramps, and ragamuffins who want to dirty their faces a little can try rubbing a finger in some brown eyeshadow or dark bronzer and smudging it onto cheeks, forehead, and nose. For a destitute look, rub some under and around your eyes, too.

A jack-in-the-box or a doll looks more toy-like with round, red cheeks. Apply red face paint with a brush to get a really clear, round shape. You could also add exaggerated, painted-on eyelashes and freckles.

Sheriffs, outlaws, and pirates need to look tough. Stubbly chins can be created by dotting on brown or black eye pencil all over the jawline and around the mouth. Scars can also be drawn on with eye pencil. For a haggard, "too long in the saddle" or "too many months at sea" look, underline your eyes with pencil.

NATIVE INDIAN. Add some war paint for an authentic touch. Check out designs in a library book or on the internet. Face paints should be applied with a flat-bristled brush that can make both broad and narrow strokes.

MONSTER. Green face paint is useful for all kinds of monstrous effects. Warts, like the ones suggested for witches, can be applied liberally, and eyes can be grotesquely outlined in unnatural colors such as red and purple. Use your imagination!

FACE MASK. Mold a mask to fit the top half of your face. It's easier to do if you enlist the help of a friend. You can take turns making masks for each other. First cover the whole area (but not your nostrils) with petroleum jelly, then lay several layers of tissue over your forehead, eyes, cheeks and top of your nose—again, not the nostrils. Moisten small pieces of gummed brown packaging tape and put them over the tissues, building them up until you have three or four layers. As you work, try to mold the mask to the contours of your face. Lift off the mask carefully and let it dry before trimming it. Cut out holes for your eyes and paint it. Use paint that matches your skin tone and add details such as eyelashes and eyebrows. When you wear it you will look "human" but oddly scary at the same time.

CLOWN. For a funny clown, start by painting the whole face white. Add a huge smile, way outside the natural lip line and extending up to the cheeks. Fill this in with red. Now draw large outlines around the eyes and exaggerated eyebrows that arch up to accentuate the smile. Round red cheeks are also a must.

For a sad clown, the basic white face is the same, but the mouth turns down and so do the eyebrows.

PIERROT. Paint only the central part of the face white, and outline this area in black. Paint black lines over eyebrows, one arching up and the other down. Outline eyes, too, and paint a tear on the cheek below the eye with the drooping brow. Paint your lips red and outline them in black with the corners turning down.

For a scarecrow or rag doll, cover your whole face and neck with yellowish-brown face paint to look like linen or burlap. Paint black lines all around the edge of your face, to look like stitching.

Frankenstein's monster will use up a lot of green face paint, so try to get a large amount at a crafts or costume store. Redefine your mouth and eyebrows with wiggly black lines, draw a lurid scar on your cheek, and stick metal or plastic bolts on each side of your neck, using eyelash glue or double-sided sticky tape.

FRANKENSTEIN HEAD. Roll up green cardboard or heavy paper to make a tube big enough to fit over your head. Cut out round holes for eyes, a zigzag hole for the mouth, and a flap for the nose. Attach bolts on either side. Decorate with paints or paper cutouts, creating thick eyebrows, heavy-lidded eyes, and a scar or two. Make hair from fringed crepe paper stuck inside the top edge of the cylinder.

Why are mummies good at keeping secrets?
—They keep things under wraps.

JACK-O'-LANTERN MASK. Cut eyeholes in a paper plate and paint the whole plate orange. Paint details in black— a triangular nose and zigzag mouth. Cut a stalk from green paper and glue in place at the top. Punch holes on both sides and thread elastic through them to hold the mask in place.

HIPPY. Use face paints and a fine brush to scatter painted flowers over your cheeks and forehead.

OLD PERSON. Sponge a pale foundation over your face and use a brown or gray eye pencil to draw in wrinkles. To do this, look in a mirror and screw up your face. Now draw lines in all the creases, around your eyes and mouth, in your forehead and chin. Relax your face and smudge the lines slightly with a fingertip.

CLEOPATRA OR KING TUTANKHAMUN. Sponge tan-colored foundation all over your face and neck. With a black eye pencil or a brush and black face paint, outline your eyes in that special, elongated way to make them look Egyptian.

Elves, pixies, leprechauns, and goblins can all make use of green face paint sponged over their faces, necks, and ears. Use black face paint and a brush to create arching eyebrows which will help to give an impish expression.

Santa needs very little makeup except for some red blusher rubbed over the cheeks and the end of the nose.

What do you call serious rocks?
—Grave stones.

If you are dressing as a skier or a sunbather, plenty of fake tan with white sunscreen strips on your mouth, nose, and forehead will look authentic.

TATTOOS. Face paints can also be used to create temporary designs on your arms and chest—or on any area of your body. You'll need a steady hand to paint them, but stick to simple designs and you'll be fine. Use black face paint and a fine brush to outline the designs and fill them in with color.

All kinds of Halloween designs can be painted onto your skin; and they are a good choice for anyone who doesn't like the feeling of being covered in makeup. Why not paint the silhouette of a black cat on your cheek, or a moon and a few stars?

What kind of makeup do monsters wear? —Mas-scare-a.

BUNNY RABBIT. Sponge white face paint over your whole face. With pink face paint and a broad brush, paint a large pink circle on either cheek, low down and close to the outer corners of your mouth. Paint pink triangles extending upward from your eyes and over each eyebrow. Using a finer brush and black face paint, outline the points of the two triangles above your eyes to make high, arching eyebrows. Then paint dots on each pink cheek with whiskers radiating outward toward your ears. Paint a little black circle on the end of your nose with a line extending down to your upper lip, and paint your upper lip black. Paint two white bunny front teeth extending down onto your lower lip and outline these in black.

SKUNK. Paint a wide white stripe of face paint down the center of your face and fill in either side with black.

PUPPY DOG. Sponge white face paint down the central part of your face, from forehead to chin. Extend this stripe outward onto your cheeks, in two large white circles. Paint the outer areas of your face with light brown face paint and use a darker shade of brown to outline your eyes and also paint bushy eyebrows. Paint a red, lolling tongue starting where your lips meet and extending down over your lower lip and halfway across your chin. Outline the tongue with black face paint, using a fine brush, and also paint your upper lip, extending a fine line up to your nose and adding a triangular blob on the tip of your nose.

BLACK AND WHITE CAT. Sponge white face paint around your mouth and chin and all around your eyes. Paint pink on the tip of your nose, around your nostrils, and on your upper lip. Paint the remaining areas of your face in black, including a black stripe down the center of your nose. Paint black dots above your upper lips and with a fine brush, add some white whiskers on your cheeks and forehead.

For a ginger cat, follow the guidelines for the black and white cat but paint the black areas in orangey-brown. For a gray or tabby cat, use gray face paint or dabs of brown and beige.

LION MAKEUP. Cover your face with a base of light orange-yellow face paint. Using a paintbrush, draw wide, white eyebrows above your natural brows and white patches on your cheeks, top lip, and chin. With black face paint and a fine brush, paint in spiky eyebrows, a triangular black nose on your nose tip, dots above your upper lip, and whiskers.

TIGER. Over a base of yellowy-orange, sponge the area around your mouth and chin, and your mouth itself, with white face paint. Add patches of white extending upwards from the eyebrows, too. Add black stripes, radiating out from the center of your face. Paint in a black nose and paint your upper lip black, extending it out at the corners. Paint black dots above your upper lips and add some whiskers.

LEOPARD. This is a variation on the tiger but sponge a yellow base on to your face and paint black spots instead of stripes.

Why does Dracula consider himself a good artist?
—Because he likes to draw blood!

LADYBUG. To match your costume, you could paint a large circle of red over the center of your face, taking in your eyes, nose, cheeks, mouth, and chin. Outline it in black, add a line down the center of your face, and paint symmetrical spots on your cheeks. If you are wearing a red, spotted costume, you could just paint your face black.

ROBOT. Face paints are available in metallic as well as standard colors. Paint your whole face, ears, and neck silver, and use black face paint and a brush to square off your eyes and mouth so they will look more mechanical.

VAMPIRE. Cover your whole face, neck, and ears with a very pale foundation or white face paint. Slick back your hair and draw in a widow's peak at the center front with a black eye pencil.

To slick down your hair, use styling wax or gel, rubbing it into your hands and then smoothing it over your hair. Comb your hair back from the face to style.

Hair gel is also good for molding. It's available in different strengths, so find the strongest to sculpt your hair or spike it up!

To create wild hair, try backcombing, strand by strand.

Hair wraps are a great way of making your hair look less than human! But don't just do one—have them all over your head, like hair extensions. It just takes time and patience. Cut a square of cardboard with a slit from one side to the center, and a small hole in the center, just big enough to slip over a thick strand of hair, close to the roots. Cut four lengths of embroidery thread, each about 4 feet (1.4 meters) long and tie them around the hair, pushing the knot close to the cardboard. Choose one of the eight threads hanging down and wrap it around the hair and the other threads, for about 1 inch (2 to 3 cm). Keep changing colors, separating different strands from the bunch you are holding, and adding the strand you have just used to the bunch. When you reach the ends of the strand of hair, tie a knot to hold all the thread ends together.

A quicker way to create mad hair is to rag it! Tear strips of colored fabric and tie each strip around a strand of hair, close to the roots. Leave the ends just hanging.

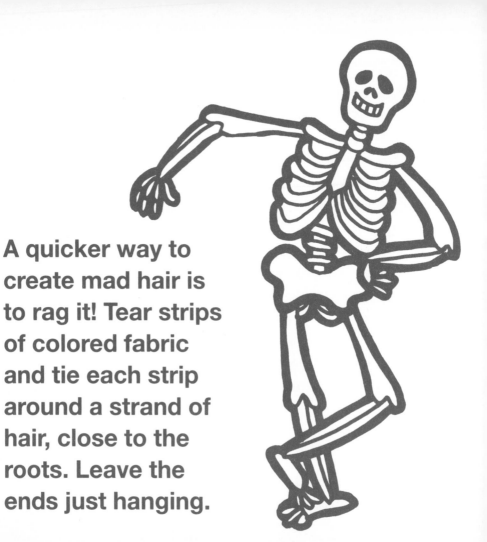

Why did the skeleton cross the road?
—To get to the Body Shop.

You can add color to your hair with colored sprays, available from novelty and costume stores. Choose one or combine several together. You can use them to stencil shapes onto your hair, too.

Why did the skeleton with one hand cross the road?
—To get to the secondhand store.

To create scars or a lumpy face, make a paste of flour and water, spread it in lumpy patches on your face, and let it dry before applying makeup over it.

For warts, stick rice crispies to your face and the backs of your hands, using eyelash glue.

For a black eye, use a cotton ball to apply diluted red face paint over your eyelid and eye socket, under your eye, and down the cheekbone just a bit. Go over your eyelid with diluted blue face paint.

**Why are monsters huge, lumpy, hairy, and ugly?
—Because if they were small, round, and smooth,
they'd be peanuts.**

BULLET HOLE. Use eyelash glue to stick a ring-shaped cereal or snack to your face—on your forehead or cheekbone. With face paint that matches your skin tone, paint it and the surrounding skin. Dip a cotton ball in diluted red face paint and dab all around the area surrounding the "wound." Squeeze a small blob of foundation inside the wound, then dab with red face paint. Add more red face paint so that it looks as if it's trickling out of the wound like blood.

COLD SORE. Stick a corn flake to the outer corner of your mouth, using eyelash glue. Paint the corn flake and the surrounding skin with face paint to match your skin tone. After that, use red face paint and a fine brush to outline the area and part of your lip with red.

A snake is a useful accessory. Buy a rubber one from a joke store or use a soft toy. Wrap it around a witch's hat or wear it as a slinky scarf. Other toy animals are useful, too. Let an owl, a mouse, or a rat poke out of a wizard's pocket, a parrot sit on a pirate's shoulder, or a black cat hang over a witch's shoulder.

WITCH'S HAT. Cut out a large circle of black cardboard, for a brim. Cut a second circle out of the center, making a hole large enough to fit snugly on your head. Make a black cardboard cone and tape this to the brim. Decorate the hat with cut-out silver stars and moons. Tape long lengths of green or purple raffia inside the cone at the back of the hat to form hair.

PAPER BAG WIG. Use a large paper bag that fits over your head. Cut a large opening in the front section of the bag for your face. Fringe the bottom of the bag and curl each strip by rolling it tightly around a pencil.

For spooky hands, try sticking on false nails. You may decide to add regular-sized ones, as part of a witch's outfit, for example. They are available from most drugstores. But look at those from party stores—they sell some really long, sharp talons!

Paint your nails—this is great for witches, vampires, aliens, and all kinds of other characters. There are so many colors to choose from—in glossy, shimmering, or sparkling textures. To steady your hand, rest your wrist on the edge of a table. Then, starting with your little finger, paint a stripe of polish, in a single stroke, down the center of your nail from the base to the tip. Quickly follow this with two more stripes to fill in both sides. Repeat with your other nails and then do the other hand. Let your nails dry before doing anything, to prevent smudging.

Look for special decorations to add designs to your painted nails—you could use small stickers—or try sprinkling your nails with glitter while the polish is still wet. A coat of clear polish will protect stickers and help to "glue" the glitter in place.

When it is time for bed, don't forget to clean off all your makeup, or you'll end up with dirty skin, irritated eyes, and smudges all over your pillowcase! Soap and water is fine for removing most makeup, especially face paints. You can also use a makeup cleanser to break down really greasy makeup, such as lipstick.

Make a sparkling necklace, fit for a king or princess, or to use as pirate treasure. String the sparkliest beads you can find onto strong thread or attach a large bead to the center of a length of chain for a regal pendant. Thrift stores and yard sales are a good place to hunt for extravagant costume jewelry at low prices.

Make a novelty necklace to suit your costume. Why not make holes in bone-shaped dog biscuits and thread them onto a leather thong or thread plastic fruits onto colorful string to be Carmen Miranda.

Why did the invisible man look in the mirror?
—To make sure he wasn't there.

Make a clothespin necklace by threading either full-sized clothespins or the tiny ones available from stationery shops onto string. Not only do they make a fun necklace but you can pin other things to them—try scraps of paper with weird predictions or Halloween sayings written on them.

Look for alphabet beads to make a necklace with a message. String them onto strong cord to spell out "Happy Halloween" or "Trick-or-treat" or whatever else you feel like saying!

Decorations
and
Party Stuff

The number one decoration for Halloween has got to be a jack-o'-lantern. Choose a ripe, unblemished pumpkin that has no bruises, cuts, or nicks.

Place the pumpkin on several layers of newspaper before carving to help steady it. Put enough newspaper around the pumpkin so you can simply drop the seeds onto it once they have been scooped out. This speeds up the cleanup— all you have to do is wrap up the newspaper, and throw it away.

If your pumpkin wobbles when it's sitting up, cut off a thin slice on the bottom to give it a level place to sit. This makes removing the seeds easier and is also a safety measure—you don't want a knife or saw to slip when you're carving the features.

Always supervise children when they are carving a pumpkin—it's too easy to make a bad mistake with a sharp instrument.

To carve a traditional jack-o'-lantern, begin by cutting a circle about 4 to 6 inches (10 to 15 cm) in diameter around the stem of the pumpkin. Use a sharp knife with a long, sturdy blade. Remove the "lid" and scoop out the pumpkin flesh. Then cut two triangular eyes, a triangular nose, and a zigzag mouth from the shell. Put a nightlight or candle inside and the glow from the flame will shine through the features you have cut out.

If your pumpkin has a particularly tough skin, you may need to use a small hand saw to cut into it. Like cutting the lid, this is a job for an adult.

If your pumpkin skin is easy to cut, use the plastic pumpkin carving tools you'll find at supermarkets and novelty stores.

When cleaning out the pumpkin, use a spoon— a large, slightly pointed one is best. Some people prefer to use a metal soup ladle to remove the flesh and seeds.

Try carving a really large pumpkin— you may find it easier to carve than a smaller one because you can reach inside with your arm.

Do not carry a pumpkin by its stem. You're bound to drop it and it will probably break into large, jagged pieces—all over the floor!

Try not to bruise the skin of your pumpkin because bruises encourage rotting and the pumpkin won't last as long.

If you don't feel comfortable cutting out the face freehand, use an artist's trick. Draw the outline of the face you want on a white plain sheet of paper, then tape the paper to the pumpkin and use a thin, sharp nail or a strong pin to prick through the outline of the face. When you take off the paper, the dotted lines will guide your hand.

You can also use a felt-tip marker to draw the features. Just cut slightly outside the lines—you'll cut off the pen marks when you cut out the features.

The standard pumpkin face has a cutout nose, but you could make a surprising change by adding a carrot nose, just as you would do to a winter snowman. Cut off as much of the stem end as necessary to make it suit the face and then, from the inside, push a wooden skewer through the pumpkin shell and into the carrot.

Add an extra touch to your jack-o'-lantern by setting a bird on top. Scour toy stores or party stores for realistic models—a crow would be just the thing.

Your pumpkin doesn't have to have a face. You could cut out star and moon shapes all over it, or make an abstract design to make the most of the light from the interior.

Metal cookie cutters and apple corers are great for creating shapes and holes in pumpkin shells.

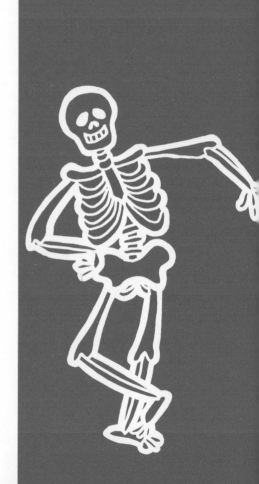

What do French skeletons say when they sit down to dinner? —Bone appetit !

To keep your pumpkin lantern from drying out, cover it with a damp hand towel when it is not on display.

If you want to make your carved pumpkin last as long as possible, let it sit for at least half an hour after you've finished carving it. With an absorbent towel, dry off all the cut surfaces as well as the entire inside of the shell and lid. Finally, seal all the cut surfaces with a protective coating of something like petroleum jelly—don't use a flammable coating as you then won't be able to light a naked flame inside the pumpkin.

You can also spray your carved pumpkin with several coats of hair spray which will seal the cut edges and make it shine—the more coats you apply, the shinier it will be. But remember—hair spray is highly flammable, so you can't put a candle inside the pumpkin.

Cutting a pumpkin can be tricky, especially for children. If you want to make sure that they are involved with the whole process, don't carve. Instead, stick trinkets and novelties all over it— star-shaped fake gems, large silver eyelets, fancy shells, stones, or the metal studs that decorate denim.

For a quick and easy pumpkin decoration, use a metallic marker pen in gold, silver or any other color to draw squiggles or designs, or why not write a Halloween message?

Why did the ghost go into the mall? —To buy some boos.

Painted pumpkins can be stunning. Acrylic paints are perfect. Paint simple stripes or swirls or, if you have the patience, a picture or scene. Use fine-tipped, felt-tipped pens to add intricate details.

Instead of using the traditional orange pumpkin, check your local supermarket or produce stand for pumpkins in unusual and different colors—white, yellow, or green.

Other vegetables can also be hollowed out and carved into lanterns—try acorn squash, butternut squash, rutabagas, and turnips.

Paint a butternut squash white and turn it into a scary ghost by painting its features with black paint or a marker.

Make a pumpkin candle holder. Cut around the stem of a small pumpkin—or alternatively you could use a decorative gourd or squash—and create a hole just the right size and shape to hold a battery-operated nightlight. Use Play-Doh or Silly Putty to hold the nightlight in place.

Scoop out holes for nightlights or candles from the stem ends of apples. Secure the lights or candles in the apples and then carefully place them in a huge washtub or half-barrel. Sit back and enjoy your display of beautiful floating lights.

Make an artistic front-porch pumpkin display. Hollow out pumpkins of various shapes, sizes, and colors. Drill holes in the skins. When you put a light inside, tiny pinpricks of light will shine through the holes. Arrange your pumpkins in a cluster near the door or on your front steps.

Paper bag lights also make a gorgeous display. Cut out designs or messages near the tops of sturdy brown paper bags, pour in a generous few handfuls of sand, and stand lighted candles inside to create a welcoming glow.

Why are ghosts such bad liars? —Because you can see right through them!

Always remember that flames are a fire hazard, even outside. Put buckets of sand and water near all the lit displays so you can quench the flames if necessary. And tempting as it might be to nip inside for just a moment, you must never leave lit candles unattended.

Make a jack-o'-lantern ball to stick on a car aerial. Just paint a lightweight ball, such as a foam ball from a craft store, with orange acrylic paint. Stick a pencil into the ball so that you have something to hold onto while you paint. Use a black felt-tip marker to draw a face. For a stem and leaves, cut shapes from green or brown craft foam, make an indentation in the top of the ball and push the stem and leaves into it. You may need to add a dab of glue to hold them in place. Remove the pencil and stick the ball on your car aerial.

To make a balloon jack-o'-lantern, blow up a round, orange balloon. Cut triangular eyes and nose and a jagged mouth from black paper and use double-sided sticky tape to attach them. Add a frill of green crepe paper around the knot of the balloon and hang it.

Candle holders are easy to make from small glass jars. To make a jack-o'-lantern jar, cut triangular eyes and nose and a wiggly mouth from masking tape and stick in place on the outside of the jar. Using glass paint from a craft store, paint the whole jar orange and, while the paint is still wet, sprinkle with glitter. Shake off the excess. When the paint is dry, peel off the masking tape. Sit a nightlight inside, on a bed of sand. The light will shine through the pumpkin face and the glitter will sparkle.

Make candlesticks from clay. Mold a lump of self-hardening clay around the base of a candle and stick Halloween decorations all over the clay.

Make a candle holder from a long clay worm. First coil it into a flat, spiral base. Continue wrapping the clay worm upward, to make the sides of a tube-shaped pot just wide enough to fit a candle and tall enough to support it. Self-hardening clay can be painted when it dries, so get out your poster paints and do some dastardly decorations. Add a coat of polyurethane varnish, or a water-based craft sealant to seal and protect your artwork.

For a Halloween wreath, decorate a plain vine wreath with Halloween decorations you've cut from paper or small figures. You can use a homemade wreath or buy one from the dried flower section of a craft store. Brush the wreath with glue and sprinkle on a lavish coat of glitter.

You could also decorate a wreath with black and orange pipe cleaners, twisted and bent to look like spiders and wiggly worms or contorted into a Halloween message such as, "Beware of ghosts" or "Evil lurks."

Make an apple wreath. Stick pieces of florists' wire into the apples. If the apples are heavy, you'll need to push two wires through them. Put the wreath base on a table and attach the apples by securely wrapping the wires you pushed through them around the wreath base. Don't just confine yourself to apples—use kumquats, starfruit, kiwis, or even passion fruits.

Place a dead branch, without leaves, in a vase—or stick it into a pumpkin, melon, or block of florists' foam. Cut out tiny Halloween designs—pumpkins, ghosts, bats, or witches—from colored paper and hang them from the branch on pieces of fine thread.

Who did the skeleton invite to his party?
—Anyone he could dig up!

Gather leaves that are dry but not too brittle and paint them on one side with acrylic paints— metallic colors look particularly effective. Let them dry and then turn them over and paint the other side. Scatter the painted leaves over your windowsills or mantelpiece, or make swags by stringing them onto some nylon thread and draping them over your doors or windows.

It's harvest time! Fill a bowl with apples, pears, and other seasonal fruit to celebrate October's bounty.

Who looks after the haunted house?
—A skeleton staff.

Spray plastic fruit black for a fiendish fruit bowl, adding patches of green "mold" by rubbing the painted fruit with green eyeshadow or dabbing with glue, sprinkling flour onto the glue, and shaking off the excess. You could even embed or attach a few rubber worms.

Find some Christmas tree balls—gold, bronze, or green ones are just right—and write scary words—"BOO!" "EEK!" "BEWARE!"—in bright, sparkly glitter glue. Hang them in strategic spots where people can come upon them suddenly.

To make Halloween window decorations, cut out designs such as bats, cats, and pumpkins. Attach them to the windows with double-sided tape or non-permanent spray adhesive.

Draw some Halloween pictures! Have fun with crayons, felt-pens or paints and proudly display them on the walls.

Use cookie cutters or stencils to make festive shapes. Put them on colored paper and trace their outlines. Then cut out the shapes. Make as many as you can and stick them all over the place—doors, windows, walls, and cupboards.

When you've finished, you can even tie the cookie cutters onto lengths of string and hang them up, too.

Tiny black paper shapes look great stuck inside a lampshade—bats are ideal and ghosts work, too.

You could thread your cutout shapes on lengths of string and suspend them from the ceiling as hanging decorations.

What did the boy ghost say to the girl ghost?
—You look boo-tiful tonight.

Theme your mobiles by grouping sets of cutouts such as bugs, or aliens, or bats.

Make magical mobiles by suspending cutouts on lengths of nylon thread, from coat hangers. The hook will make it easy to hang your mobile from the edge of a shelf, a nail, or the branch of a tree.

Make a snake mobile by cutting cardstock into a circle and then, starting at an edge, cut it into a spiral. Pull it out and it will look like a snake, especially if you make one end thicker than the other and draw a pair of eyes on the thicker end. You could also glue fangs and a forked tongue onto the head, cut from a scrap of paper. Hang the snake on a length of nylon thread.

Thread plastic tops from water, juice, or milk bottles, circles cut from heavy construction paper, and circles cut from aluminum foil onto a piece of strong thread. Use a darning needle to pierce each one in turn. When you have enough to make a long snake body, add a head made from a polystyrene ball or a large bead and add a forked tongue cut from red paper. Hang this up in a breezy spot and it will not only look good, but it will rattle too!

Cut shapes from sheets of craft foam—ghosts and pumpkin heads. You should be able to get three ghosts or four pumpkins from a standard sized sheet of foam. Use a glue stick to glue on googly eyes and facial features cut from black paper. Twirl a pipe cleaner around a pencil to make a spiral hook for hanging up your spooky shapes. Hang them from a length of string, from door handles— anywhere you like!

Witches and wizards will want plenty of sparkling stars to decorate their homes this Halloween. Cut star shapes from thick cardboard, brush glue all over them and sprinkle on plenty of glitter. Use different colors for multicolored effects! Leave to dry thoroughly before arranging on walls, windows, and tables.

Cut out moon and star shapes from cardstock and stick them on the wall to form a Halloween constellation. Why not cut out photographs of yourself and other family members and stick these in the centers of the stars?

What do you call a skeleton
in a closet?
—Last year's hide-and-seek winner.

Have you got any family
portraits on the walls?
Whether they are photographs
or paintings, why not dress
them up a bit (temporarily, of
course) by sticking on false
beards and glasses or by
giving them evil expressions,
using cutout pieces of paper?

A spider hanging from the ceiling makes a particularly scary Halloween decoration. Make a medium-sized spider quickly and easily from a polystyrene ball, painted black. Push black pipe cleaners for legs through the ball and glue on plastic googly eyes. Hang a piece of transparent nylon fishing line from the ceiling to attach it to.

For a bigger spider, use a black balloon. Make legs from old black tights stuffed with newspapers and taped in place. Add cutout eyes and fangs, too.

For a giant spider, fill a black plastic garbage bag with crumpled newspaper and seal the top. Make legs from black plastic pipe. Plastic plates or old car headlights make fantastic eyes. Set it up on the lawn or the front steps unless you have a tree where you want to hang it.

Empty cereal boxes make great gravestones. Paint the empty box with poster paint in a medium shade of gray—mix black and white paint to get the right shade. You'll need a lighter and a darker shade of gray. Create a mottled stone effect by using a sponge to dab the gray paints onto the box. When the paint is dry, use black paint or a marker to add an epitaph. You'll need to weigh it down, so fill a plastic bag with pebbles or sand and put the bag into the bottom of the box. Put a tarp on the lawn and mound soil or chipped bark mulch over it. Bury the bottom 2 inches (5 cm) of your gravestone into the mound.

You can also make a gravestone from polystyrene. You can often find thick polystyrene in packaging, especially around electrical appliances. Cut out the gravestone with a bread knife and use a sharp-pointed instrument to carve an inscription. Use spray paint to make it gray.

Make a scarecrow to stand in your garden—it could scare away trick-or-treaters as well as birds! Make a head from an old fabric bag or cushion cover stuffed with straw and set it on top of a tall, sturdy stick. Then tie a stick across the upright pole to create arms. Dress your scarecrow in old clothes stuffed with straw or crumpled plastic bags. Straw hair, a painted face, and a hat create a real character.

You can also make a little "indoor" scarecrow, like the outdoor one but on a smaller scale, using smaller sticks and dolls' clothes. Stick it in a plant pot or window box.

What did the skeleton say when he walked into a bar?
—Ouch!!! It was an iron bar!

Make a rattling scarecrow with a body, arms, and legs made from empty rolls of toilet paper, paper towels, plastic wrap, and so on. Tape the rolls together or thread them onto string so they have some movement. Push straw or shredded paper into the ends of the rolls but let it peek out at the ends. Hang the scarecrow in a breezy spot.

Make place mats from large paper shapes—ghosts cut from white paper, cats or bats cut from black paper, pumpkins cut from orange paper, or a scary monster face cut from green paper. Decorate with cutout features made from colored paper scraps. For a wipe-clean surface, take your paper place mats to the nearest copy store and get them laminated.

Another paper cutout idea is a doorknob hanger. Cut Halloween designs from colored card or paper. A ghost is a particularly good shape. Cut a round hole out of the shape so you can slip it over the doorknob and add a message such as "at home to ghosts" or "no entry to spooks." You can even get your doorknob hanger laminated, too.

For a different doorknob hanger, stick two different colored rectangles of cardstock back to back to make it reversible. Cut a circular hole at the top so you can slip it over a door handle. Put a different message on each side. On one side you could add a scary photo of yourself making a nasty face, to frighten everyone away. On the other, you could write a welcoming greeting and stick on a smiley photo.

Warning bells. When you are up to tricks, you don't want unwelcome visitors bursting in on you. Thread bells onto a length of ribbon and tie the ends together to make a loop for hanging. Hang it on the inside of your bedroom door.

To make a paper napkin ghost, place a cotton ball in the center of a napkin and tie a piece of white string around the "neck." Using a black marker, draw a spooky face on your ghost. Tape a length of "invisible" thread from the top of its head and hang it in a draft so it flutters in the breeze.

For floating ghosts, drape helium-filled balloons with squares of white cloth. Draw on eyes with a black marker.

If you want to bring your floating ghosts down to earth, tie lengths of string or ribbon to the necks of the helium balloons and tie the other ends to weights—try tying the ends to the stems of little pumpkins. Hide the pumpkins in the bushes by the front door to scare your visiting trick-or-treaters.

Buy plastic spiders' webs from a party shop and place them in the corners of the ceiling and across the tops of doorways.

Empty canisters from cocoa, baking powder, and breadcrumbs make great containers for Halloween parties. Cover them in paper and label them as "deadly poison," "eye of newt," or "evil slime." Fill them with treats and set them around the party room.

You could also label containers as "candy" and "treats" but fill them with cotton balls or shredded tissue paper as a surprise for prying fingers.

Make false labels for the cans and jars in the pantry. Label jars of pasta sauce "bloody guts" and cat food "shredded mice." Use your imagination.

Put bugs in the fridge! Buy edible gummy worms, spiders, and other bugs. Wrap a couple of worms around the neck of a ketchup bottle, drape a spider from the crisper, and set the other bugs in strategic places all over the house!

Buy plastic rats, spiders, and snakes from a toy or joke store and put them in corners, under tables, on top of the fridge—all over the place. When the lights are dim, they look quite real!

Plastic spiders, available from joke stores, can be placed in the fruit bowl, on lampshades, and in locations all over the house—ready to be discovered by the unaware.

What is a ghost's favorite party game? —Hide-and-shriek.

Cover your walls temporarily with dark-colored paper or lengths of fabric— black, deep red, navy blue, or bottle green.

Candles, soft lighting, and heavily shaded lamps not only lower the light levels but also make creatures passing in front of them cast long, eerie shadows.

Replace your regular light bulbs with colored bulbs—red, blue, and green, to cast an eerie glow.

For a further eerie effect, hang glow-in-the-dark bats from the ceiling and watch what happens when you turn out the lights!

Clear out your fireplace and fill with orange and black pillar candles in various shapes and sizes.

If your curtains or blinds don't block out enough light, cover the windows with blankets, black garbage bags, or aluminum foil to block it out completely.

When your house is dark or dimly lit, for safety's sake, put some reflective tape on the doorknobs so people can easily find their way out.

Who did Frankenstein take to the party? —His ghoul friend.

Cover the furniture with lengths of inexpensive black fabric. You can create the right atmosphere while also protecting the upholstery from sticky fingers and little faces covered in makeup.

Get lengths of real or fake ivy and wind it around chair backs, table legs, and other furniture for an eerily overgrown look. Add tall plants and hanging baskets to create an overgrown atmosphere.

For a cobwebby effect that will give your whole house an abandoned appearance, pull cotton batting apart into spidery threads and drape them across furniture and doorways.

Why do demons and ghouls get on with each other?
—Because demons are a ghoul's best friend.

Don't just wear a spooky mask this Halloween—hang a few on the walls, too.

Lay the table with elegant china and silver, candelabras, and trays or baskets filled with costume jewelry.

Use black or orange cotton as a tablecloth during the Halloween period.

Printed tablecloths are easy to make with rubber stamps. Find some with Halloween figures and use black ink over an orange cloth or orange ink over a black cloth.

Use tubes of dimensional paint in white or silver to draw spiders' webs on black fabric, and then drape the fabric around the room.

If you haven't any black or orange china, buy orange and black paper plates, cups, and napkins.

At dinnertime on Halloween, put a trick-or-treat bag at each place setting. Even if you're not having a party, it will create a festive atmosphere.

Having the right music playing helps to create a suitable atmosphere for Halloween. A plaintive piano sonata or sad instrumental tune will do.

Let a plastic spider or other Halloween joke item peek out from under everyone's plate at breakfast.

Potted plants can help to create the look of a haunted mansion, especially rubber plants and aspidistras (parlor palms). Place them on the piano, if you have one, or on a small table covered with a dark cloth.

Lilies are beautiful but can look quite dismal, as they are traditionally associated with funerals. Arrange waxy white lilies with tall stems in a tall jar.

Homemade paper flowers are usually colorful and pretty—but not if they have green or black petals! Crepe paper is a good material for these because you can stretch each petal into shape. For the flower center, cut a strip of paper into a fringe, wind it around the end of a stick, and fray out the fronds. Then cut individual petals and stretch each one to make it curl. Tape the petals to the stick and wind a long strip of green crepe paper around the base of the flower— hiding the tape—and wrap it around the stick. Display your beastly blooms in a vase or tape them around the edges of a mirror.

Make paper garlands. Cut six-pointed star or flower shapes from orange and black tissue paper. With a glue stick, dab a spot of glue onto the tips of three of the points of a single star or flower and stick another star or flower on top. Now dab glue on the other three—the unglued points—and stick another shape on top. Continue like this, gluing alternate sets of three points, until the garland is the right size.

What goes, "Ha ha ha ha"—thud? —A zombie laughing its head off!

Cover buckets with orange paper that's held in place with double-sided tape. Fill them with Halloween treats or autumnal arrangements of flowers and twigs. Decorate the outside with black paper cutouts.

Buckets can also be swathed in orange or black fabric and used as temporary planters. Just stand potted plants inside.

Instead of fresh flowers, display a vase of dead roses. Buy fresh roses a week or so before Halloween and stand them in a vase with very little water. Leave them until the water evaporates—they will dry in place. After Halloween, store them in a shoe box and you can bring them out again next year.

Make a big display of dead twigs and branches or even potted dead plants. You could spray them with black paint for an even more depressing effect!

Do you hang up your stocking on the fireplace at Christmas? Well why not hang up a pair of smelly socks at Halloween?

Set the scene. Recreate a tableau from a favorite movie or book. Use films such as *Ghostbusters*, *The Witches*, or *The Nightmare Before Christmas* as your inspiration.

Recreate the famous scene from *The Wizard of Oz* where the house has fallen on the wicked witch. Stuff crumpled newspapers into a pair of red and white striped socks, add a pair of high-heeled shoes, and let them stick out from under a sofa.

Where does a ghost go on Saturday night? —Anywhere he can boo-gie.

What is a vampire's favorite celebration? —Fangsgiving.

Spread some crispy dry cereal under a rug. When people walk over it, they will get a surprise from the crunching sounds underfoot.

Create a crime scene on your front path, driveway, or even inside. Get someone to lie on the floor and draw around their body with white chalk. Drape yellow paper around it and write "Do Not Enter—Crime Scene" with a black marker at intervals along the paper.

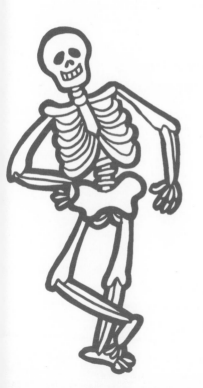

Leave a "dead body" lying around. Stuff old clothes—a pair of trousers and a shirt—and place these on the floor in a curled-up, lying position. Add a hat, shoes, and gloves for further realism. You could even stick a knife in the chest and squirt tomato ketchup around it.

Put a fake hand behind the toilet (buy it from a novelty store). Or let a pair of fake feet poke out from a floor-length curtain.

Why are monsters wrinkly?
—Have you ever tried to iron a monster?

Stick false fingernails onto latex gloves, fill them with popcorn, and tie up the wrists with red ribbon. Leave these "severed hands" lying around the house.

While you are decorating your own house, why not decorate your dolls' house too? Use miniature versions of your favorite decorations—wooden beads painted to look like jack-o'-lanterns, black and orange swags, and little ghosts flying around in every room!

What type of monster really loves dance music?
—The boogieman!

For a miniature haunted house, you could also decorate a bird house. Buy a plain, unpainted wooden bird house from a craft store or garden center. Paint it to look like a haunted mansion and set tiny ghosts, made from paper or fabric, at the windows and the chimney.

And don't forget the dog house—decorate it with a few paper ghosts and leave some bones lying around the entrance!

Stick windmills in the flower beds or window boxes outside your house and they will whirr and rattle when the wind catches them. Buy plastic windmills or make your own from stiff paper.

Make Halloween wind chimes to frighten neighbors and visiting trick-or-treaters. Tie objects onto strong thread and hang several strings together—the objects will bump and clatter into each other in the wind. Suitable objects include old cutlery, seashells, bits of broken jewelry, and bottle tops. See what you have lying around, but make sure that a few of the objects are shaped to catch the wind.

Fill the bathtub with water and float lighted black candles and plastic spiders in the water.

Why didn't the skeleton dance at the party?
—He had no body to dance with.

Paper chains are easy to make. Cut black and orange paper into long strips—about 8 x $\frac{3}{4}$ inch (20 x 2 cm). Glue one strip into a ring. Slip one end of the next strip into the ring and glue it together to make a second ring—you now have the beginning of a chain. Continue in this fashion to make a chain of the correct length.

Make party swags in Halloween colors. Cut triangles out of orange and black paper and fold and glue the long edges over a string attached to the ceiling or a doorway.

Make swags to hang outside. Cut triangles from black and orange plastic bags, loop the top edge of each flag over strong twine and use electrical tape to attach them.

Make a string of jack-o'-lanterns to hang around the room—over windows, on the mantelpiece, and across the ceiling. Draw pumpkin shapes on orange paper. Give them long stems and draw black jack-o'-lantern faces with black marker. Fold each stem over a length of string and hold it in place with glue or sticky tape.

In Mexico, they celebrate the Day of the Dead in style. Make your own Mexican-style flags from brightly colored tissue paper. Cut tissue paper into 8 x 6-inch rectangles (20 x 15 cm). Fold each one in half, then in half again, and make lots of little cuts in it. When you unfold the paper, you'll see the pattern of cuts. If you have scissors with fancy blades, use them to trim the edges. Fold and tape the top edge of each flag over a piece of string and hang between trees in your yard or from the walls or ceilings.

Make a witch's cauldron from papier mâché. With some clever paint effects, you can make it look like metal! Stick it in the middle of the table at Halloween and fill it with goodies! Begin by blowing up a balloon to the size you want your finished cauldron to be. Coat it almost entirely with at least eight layers of papier mâché, letting it dry between the fourth and fifth layer—this allows it to dry more quickly after you've added the last layer. When the completed papier mâché ball is dry, stick a needle into the balloon to burst it. You'll have a thick papier mâché shell. Trim the edge to make it smooth. Glue three corks or wooden blocks to make legs on the bottom. Paint the cauldron, inside and out, with black paint. Then, using a scrap of paper or cloth, rub the surface with a small amount of metallic gold or bronze paint. Cut a metal hanger for a handle and bore through the top of the cauldron with a skewer to attach it.

Make a pumpkin head in the same way as you did the cauldron—but don't put legs on it, of course! Instead, glue a lid from an old jelly or mustard jar onto the bottom to give it a flat base. Dab different shades of orange and red all over it to create a mottled effect. Let that dry before adding a gruesome face. Use it as a table centerpiece, with a small flashlight inside, or carry it with you when you go trick-or-treating.

Make a little sock ghost—ideal for decorating the mantelpiece or sideboard. Cut the foot off an old white sock—you'll use the ankle and leg part for the ghost's body. Stitch the raw edges together and stuff your ghost's body with batting or foam chips. Cut a circle from the remaining part of the sock, and use it to cover a jelly jar lid—you can glue the edges of the fabric inside the lid. Then tuck the ribbing at the base of the ghost's body inside the lid, fold the edge to the inside for a hem, and stitch it to the fabric covering the lid. This makes a base for the ghost so it can stand on its own. To make the head, tie a piece of yarn or thread about a third of the way down the body, tightly enough to separate the two sections. Cut the eyes and mouth from a piece of black felt and glue them in place.

How does a girl vampire flirt?
—She bats her eyes.

Food

Whether you are preparing food for your family, for friends, or for a huge party, you will need some special Halloween recipes. These could be traditional Halloween fare, your own crazy concoctions, or, quite frankly, familiar favorites with novelty names!

When does a ghost have breakfast?
—In the moaning.

SOUL CAKES. These are the traditional reward given to ancient trick-or-treaters. Cream together $\frac{3}{4}$ cup, packed (175 g) butter and the same amount of sugar, then beat in 3 egg yolks, one at a time. Sift 4 cups (460 g) all-purpose flour and a pinch of mixed spice into the mixture and mix well. Fold in $\frac{1}{2}$ cup (75 g) currants. Mix to form a soft dough, adding a little milk if the mixture seems too dry. Divide the dough into 16 lumps and shape each one into a cake. Place, spaced well apart, on a greased baking sheet and mark each one with a cross. Bake at 350°F (180°C/gas 4) for 10 to 15 minutes.

BAKED APPLES WITH WORMS. Core 12 large eating apples and place a knob of unsalted butter and 1 teaspoon jelly into each cavity. Bake at 350°F (180°C/gas 4) for 35 to 45 minutes, until tender but not too soft. Allow to cool for 15 minutes, then serve with a gummy worm stuck into each one.

SATAN'S SALSA. Dice 2 tomatoes, 2 scallions, and half a cucumber as small as you can. Put them in a bowl and stir in 2 tablespoons tomato relish and 2 tablespoons tomato ketchup, some salt, and pepper. Snip fresh herbs—coriander, mint, or parsley—into small pieces and stir in just before serving this colorful dip with tortilla chips or potato chips. You can also spoon it over burgers or hot dogs.

Why are school cooks cruel? —Because they batter fish and beat eggs.

GHOSTIE LOLLIPOPS. Keep the wrapper on your lollipop and place a square of white tissue over it. Tie a bow of string or white ribbon around the top of the stick to hold the tissue in place. Decorate the tissue to look like a ghost by using a black marker to make eyes on it.

Do zombies eat popcorn with their fingers?
—No, they eat the fingers separately.

GHOSTLY SAND-WITCHES. Make your favorite sandwich, using white bread, then use a Halloween ghost-shaped cookie cutter to stamp out a shape from the middle of the sandwich. Add raisins or slices of black olives for eyes.

DRACULA'S PUNCH. In a large punch bowl, combine 6 cups (1.5 liters) cranberry juice and the same quantity of flavored sparkling water. Add 1 blood orange, cut into 12 slices, and just before serving, add some ice cubes. (12 servings.)

WITCHES' FINGERS. Make a cookie dough by mixing 10 tablespoons (125 g) softened butter with 1 cup (125 g) powdered sugar, 1 egg, and 1 teaspoon almond extract. Beat in $2\frac{1}{4}$ scant cups (250 g) all-purpose flour with 1 teaspoon baking powder and 1 teaspoon salt. Cover and refrigerate for 30 minutes. Divide the dough into about 30 pieces, then mold each piece into the shape of a finger with knobbly knuckles. Press half a blanched almond firmly into one end of each finger to make a nail. Place on a lightly greased baking sheet and bake, in batches, at 325°F (150°C/gas 3) for 20 to 25 minutes, or until golden.

What do you call someone who puts poison in their victim's cornflakes?
—A cereal killer.

DEVIL DOGS. Make hot dogs in buns as usual. Combine equal quantities of tomato ketchup and mustard with a dash of Worcestershire sauce and a few drops of Tabasco sauce and dribble this spicy mixture over each one for hot dogs with a kick!

BARBECUED BONES. Start with 2 pounds (900 g) chicken wings. Cut each chicken wing in half by snipping through the joint in the middle. In a large bowl, mix together half a can of cola, 2 tablespoons sugar, 4 tablespoons ketchup, 1 tablespoon mustard, and 1 tablespoon Worcestershire sauce. Add the prepared chicken wings and leave to marinate for 1 hour. Heat the oven to 400°F (200°C/gas 6) and arrange the chicken pieces in a single layer on a baking pan. Cook for 20 minutes, then turn each one over and cook for an additional 20 minutes. To check that the chicken is cooked, pierce with a skewer or the tip of a knife. The juices should run clear. Eat hot or cold. If you can't get chicken wings, use chicken drumsticks. (Because drumsticks are slightly larger, they will need another

When do cannibals cook their victims?
—On Fry-day.

VAMPIRE SAUCE. Chop 1 large onion and 2 ribs of celery into very small pieces. Heat the oil in a saucepan over medium heat and stir frequently while you cook the onion and celery for 10 minutes, or until soft and golden. Chop 8 ripe tomatoes or use a 28-ounce (794 g) can of plum tomatoes. Add the tomatoes to the pan and cook for 2 more minutes, then stir in 4 tablespoons tomato purée and 4 tablespoons water. Cook the sauce for 10 minutes, then add salt and pepper. This sauce can be used with pasta or as a pizza topping. The recipe makes enough for four servings and it can be kept in a covered container in the refrigerator for up to three days and reheated as necessary.

SNAIL SANDWICHES. Spread 2 tablespoons cream cheese mixed with a squeeze of tomato ketchup (to make it pink) or green ketchup (to make it green) over a large flour tortilla or a wrap. Use vegetable wraps for different colors. Roll it up tightly and cut into slices before arranging on a serving plate to form the snails' shells. Add a pickle "body" to each one.

What kind of pasta do ghosts like to eat?
—Spooketti.

SUGAR PUMPKIN COOKIES. Make up a batch of your favorite sugar cookie dough, roll it out, and cut pumpkin-shaped cookies with a template you've made from cardboard or a store-bought cookie cutter. When baked and cooled, spread with icing that you've tinted orange with a few drops of red and yellow food coloring, and sprinkle on some sugar while the icing is still wet. Add stalks and leaves made from green gummy worms, and add eyes, noses, and mouths you've cut from other gummy or jelly candies.

Why wasn't there any food left after the monsters' party?
—Because everyone was a goblin!

GINGER GHOSTS. Place 7 tablespoons (90 g) butter, a packed $\frac{1}{2}$-cup (125 g) sugar, and 2 tablespoons corn (golden) syrup in a saucepan and heat very gently, stirring with a wooden spoon, until melted and mixed. Sift packed $1\frac{1}{2}$ cups (175 g) all-purpose flour, 2 tablespoons ginger, and 1 tablespoon baking soda into a large bowl. Stir in the melted ingredients to make a firm dough. Roll out the dough on a floured board, to $\frac{1}{4}$-inch (5 mm) thick. Use a knife or cutter to cut out ghost shapes and place on greased baking sheets. Bake at 350°F (180°C/gas 4) for 10 to 12 minutes, then transfer to a wire rack and let cool. Spread ghost cookies with white icing, then use black icing—you can buy this, ready-to-use, in little tubes—to add eyes and screeching mouths.

CHOCOLATE SPIDERS. Cut black licorice strings into 3-inch (8 cm) pieces and push eight of them into a chocolate-covered marshmallow. Make two googly eyes from mini marshmallows skewered into place with short pieces of leftover licorice string.

SWAMP SLIME. Make a package of lime gelatin, according to the directions on the package but add about 10 percent (about $\frac{1}{8}$ cup to 2 cups) extra water so it is quite sloppy when set. Divide half of the gelatin between small, clear plastic cups and place these in the refrigerator until set. Add a few sweet jelly worms and bugs, purchased from a sweet shop, to each cup, then top up with the remaining gelatin and refrigerate until set.

How do vampires invite each other out for lunch? —Do you want to go out for a bite?

BLACK CATS AND BATS. If you are lucky enough to have some suitable molds—such as cats or bats or other Halloween characters—you can make black gelatin. Just add a few drops of black food coloring to a blackcurrant-flavored gelatin after you have made it up according to the package directions and then pour it into the molds.

What do you get when you cross a black cat with a lemon.
—A sour puss.

FRENCH TOAST TOMBSTONES. Spread eight slices of white bread with cream cheese, add a blob of jelly in the center of each, and top with a second slice of bread. Whisk 4 eggs in a large bowl with a little less than $\frac{1}{2}$ cup (100 ml) of milk. Heat a large frying pan over medium heat and melt 1 tablespoon butter into it. Dip the sandwiches in the egg mixture and fry for 3 to 4 minutes on each side, until golden brown. Sprinkle with powdered sugar and serve for breakfast.

FLOATING HANDS. Wash a surgical glove thoroughly and fill it with water. Close it with a rubber band and freeze until solid. Use a craft or mat knife to slit the rubber. Peel the glove off the frozen hand before floating it in a bowl of very cold punch.

DIRT AND WORMS. Crumble chocolate cake and place the crumbles in individual serving bowls. Top with some gummy worms, drizzle with chocolate sauce or syrup, and dust with cocoa powder.

CHOCOLATE ORANGE JACK-O'-LANTERNS. Slice the tops off oranges and scoop out the contents. Carve a scary face and fill your orange jack-o'-lantern with chocolate ice cream. Place in the freezer until ready to serve.

What did the skeleton order at the restaurant? —Spare ribs.

FRUIT CAULDRON. Cut a slice from the base of a watermelon so it will stand up, then cut a round hole—about the size of a saucer—in the top. Scoop out the seeds and some of the flesh to leave a thick shell, then fill this with a salad made from chunks of fresh fruit—bananas, peaches, strawberries, grapes, or whatever you have available.

BUGS IN ICE. Freeze ice cubes with raisins in them—they look just like frozen bugs!

PASTA WORMS WITH BUGS. Break spaghetti into 3-inch (7.5 cm) pieces and cook in plenty of boiling, salted water for 8 minutes, or according to the directions on the package. Drain the pasta and immediately stir in a tablespoon of butter, a generous glug of olive oil, some finely grated Parmesan cheese, and handfuls of black olives and mini pickles.

MUMMIES' BANDAGES. Use a vegetable peeler to cut 4 large carrots and 2 zucchini into ribbons and toss with a generous few tablespoons of bottled Caesar salad dressing. Arrange on a serving platter and scatter with shavings of Parmesan cheese.

What do ghosts pour over their meat and vegetables?
—Grave-y.

Home-baked bread can be shaped into novelty loaves and rolls for Halloween. To make a basic bread dough, put 4 scant cups (450 g) all-purpose white flour, 1 teaspoon salt, 1 teaspoon sugar, and 1 packet of active dry yeast in a large bowl. Mix these together with a wooden spoon, then stir in $1\frac{1}{2}$ cups (325 ml) warm water. The dough should be soft and sticky. Knead it on a floured surface for about 5 to 10 minutes. It should become less sticky and quite springy. Place the dough in a lightly oiled plastic bag in a bowl, or on a tray and leave it to rise in a warm place for about 40 minutes. It should double in size. Knead the dough again, for about 5 minutes, then form it into a loaf or some rolls.

HEDGEHOG ROLLS. Divide the basic bread dough (see p184) into 12 equal pieces and shape into rolls. To make them into hedgehogs, pinch one end into a pointed snout, push peppercorns or cloves in place to make eyes, then make little snips in the dough with the points of a pair of scissors to form prickles. Place the rolls on a baking sheet. Beat an egg with 1 teaspoon sugar and 1 teaspoon water, and brush this over the surface of the dough. Cover the rolls with a cloth and leave them in a warm place for 30 to 40 minutes to rise again. Bake them for 20 minutes in a 450°F (230°C/gas 8) oven. The rolls are cooked when they are a golden color and sound hollow when you tap them on the bottom. Transfer them to a wire rack and let them cool slightly before serving.

BREAD OF THE DEAD. Shape bread dough into skulls and crossed bones to make Mexican-style *pan de muertos*. Like the hedgehog rolls, bake them for about 20 minutes and then, while they are still hot, brush them with a glaze made by melting a scant $\frac{1}{4}$-cup (50 g) sugar in 1 tablespoon orange juice.

SCARY FACE PIZZA. To make pizza dough, foll
recipe for basic bread dough (see p184), replacing
sugar with 2 tablespoons olive oil. Knead the dough
10 minutes, place in an oiled plastic bag in a bowl in a
warm place for about 40 minutes, until it doubles in size,
then shape into two rounds and add your toppings.
Spread each one with about 2 to 3 tablespoons tomato
sauce. Add triangular slices of cheese to form cheeks,
nose and chin, then add pimento-stuffed olives for eyes
and a snarling mouth cut from a slice of red pepper.
You can use all kinds of ingredients—capers, anchovies,
slices of tomato, and so on—to create your own
gruesome faces. Bake the pizzas for 15 minutes in a hot
oven until the cheese has melted and the edges of the
dough are crisp and golden.

Why should a skeleton drink plenty of milk?
—It's good for the bones.

Cover a chocolate cookie with
…nd stand a chocolate ice cream
…in the spread. Where the
…around the sides, form a
…ie of small candies.

…ow the
…g the
…s for

WITCHES' BROOMS. Using chocolate finger cookies for the handles, cut black licorice strings into 2-inch (5 cm) pieces for bristles, and tie a bundle of them in place at one end with a piece of red licorice string.

WITCH'S BREW PUNCH. Mix cranberry juice, frozen orange juice (with pulp), and ginger ale. Add green and blue food coloring until it turns a disgusting gray color.

BLOOD, SWEAT AND TEARS. Put some ice cubes into a tall glass and fill almost to the brim with tomato juice. Add a squeeze of lemon juice and as much Tabasco sauce as you dare!

For a warm and wicked Halloween drink, pour 4 cups (1 liter) of grape juice into a saucepan. Add a cinnamon stick, 8 cardamom pods, 1 teaspoon grated nutmeg, 2 tablespoons brown sugar, and the juice of half a lemon. Heat to the simmering point. Cover, remove from the heat, and leave for 10 minutes before serving to let the spices infuse.

What does a vampire never order in a restaurant?

A stake!

YEBALLS. Remove shells from hard-cooked eggs and cut the eggs in half, crosswise. Scoop out the yolks, mix with cream cheese, and use the mixture to refill the cavities. Add a pimento-stuffed olive to each one. For a bloodshot effect, decorate the egg whites with red food coloring applied with a cocktail stick.

GROSS GUACAMOLE. This is really a version of the Mexican-style dip guacamole. Skin 2 ripe avocados and remove the pits. Mash the flesh in a bowl. Stir in 1 chopped tomato or 1 tablespoon of tomato relish, 2 or 3 chopped scallions, some salt, and the juice of 1 lime. For a bit of spice, add a few drops of Tabasco or hot pepper sauce.

NUTTY POPCORN. Cover a baking sheet with a thick layer of plain, unsalted popcorn; scatter a handful of peanuts and a sprinkling of sesame seeds on top. In a small saucepan over low heat, combine 3 tablespoons honey, 3 tablespoons butter, and a pinch of cinnamon, stirring until the butter melts. Pour over the popcorn and bake at 325°F (150°C/gas 3) for 20 minutes.

What do you get when you cross a skeleton with a jar of peanut butter?
—Extra-crunchy peanut butter.

MERINGUE GHOSTIES. Whisk two egg whites until they are stiff, then whisk in a scant $\frac{1}{4}$-cup (50 g) sugar. Fold in another scant $\frac{1}{4}$-cup (50 g) sugar, then place spoonfuls of the mixture on a baking sheet. Make each little pile tall and slightly pointed on top, so it looks like a tiny ghost. Bake for about 2 hours in an oven at its lowest possible setting. When the meringues are cooled, you can add eyes with chocolate icing, if you like.

LITTLE CUPCAKE CAULDRON. Turn a cupcake upside down and use a teaspoon to scoop out a hole from the center, leaving a fairly thick shell. Using a small knife, apply a thick layer of chocolate spread to the outside of the cake. Stand the cupcake cauldron on a plate and stick the ends of a piece of licorice string into the sides of the cake to form a handle. Now fill the cauldron with green jelly, a few gummy worms, and a scattering of silver cake ball candies.

Make a gingerbread house, like the witch's house in the fairytale Hansel and Gretel. Make walls from squares of ginger cookie (use the recipe for ginger ghosts from p178), joined with icing and decorated with candies for roof tiles, bricks, window frames, and so on. Place it on a cake board sprinkled with shredded coconut colored with green food coloring to represent grass.

What do you put on top of a ghost's ice-cream sundae? —Whipped scream.

GOOD FAIRY CAKES. Sift packed $1\frac{1}{4}$ cups (150 g) self-rising flour into a large bowl. Add 8 tablespoons soft margarine, a scant $\frac{1}{2}$-cup (100 g) sugar, 2 eggs, and 2 drops vanilla extract and beat with a wooden spoon until evenly blended. Spoon the mixture into tiny paper cases and bake at 350°F (180°C/gas 4) for 15 minutes, until the cakes are springy to the touch. Place on a wire rack and let cool. Make icing by mixing 2 cups (250 g) powdered sugar with 2 to 3 teaspoons water and a few drops of food coloring, and spread a little icing on top of each cake. Then add sugar strands, cake ball candies, and other edible decorations.

STENCILED CAKES. Place a paper stencil on the flat surface of a plain cake or cookie. Make your own stencil by cutting out a suitable Halloween shape—a cat, perhaps, or a bat? If the cake is dark-colored, sift white powdered sugar onto the cake; if it is light-colored, sift cocoa powder all over the cutout area of the stencil. Lift the paper to reveal the design.

SCABS. Using a potato peeler or vegetable mandolin, slice raw potatoes, carrots, sweet potatoes, beets, and parsnips into very thin slices. Pat dry on paper towels and deep-fry in batches until crisp. Drain on kitchen paper before serving.

What kind of coffee does Dracula always drink?
—Decoffinated—with plenty of scream!

SPIDER CAKES. Spread a thick layer of white icing on top of a cupcake and draw a spiral of brown or black icing (using ready-made icing squeezed straight from the tube) onto it. To make a web design, pull the point of a cocktail stick from the center of the cupcake to the outside, like the spokes of a wheel, and from the outside to the center. Stick a hard black candy in the center and add short pieces of black licorice strings for legs,

SWEET CORN CRITTERS. Mix a 15-ounce (400 g) can of corn kernels, drained, with 1 egg, 3 to 4 tablespoons flour, and a little salt and pepper. The mixture should be quite thick, like porridge. If it seems too thin, add a little more flour. Heat 2 tablespoons oil in a frying pan over medium heat and using a large spoon or ladle, drop small puddles of mixture into the pan. Cook for 1 or 2 minutes, until you can see the edges of the underside of the fritters turning golden brown, then turn them over with a spatula and cook for another minute or two. Remove the fritters from the pan and repeat until all the mixture has been used up. To turn the fritters into critters, arrange on a serving plate and add sliced black olives for eyes and a slice of red pepper for a mouth!

ONION BREATH. Put plenty of raw onion in this dip—it tastes great and you can terrorize everyone by threatening to breathe over them afterward! Mix together 2 tablespoons each of natural yogurt, cream cheese, and mayonnaise. Add 1 teaspoon mustard and mix really well with a fork or whisk. Stir in 2 finely chopped onions and season with salt and pepper. Serve with potato or tortilla chips or spread onto pieces of toast.

Why did the monster eat a light bulb?
—Because he fancied a light snack.

PIRANHA BITES. Peel and boil 4 potatoes until they are soft. Drain and mash with 1 tablespoon butter and 2 tablespoons milk. Mix in a 7-ounce (200 g) can of salmon, 2 eggs, 1 tablespoon tomato ketchup, and a little salt and pepper. Divide the mixture into 16 equal portions and mold each one into a little fish-shaped cake. Beat an egg in a shallow dish and fill another dish with dry breadcrumbs. Dip each fish cake into the egg so it is coated all over and then coat in the breadcrumbs. Heat 2 tablespoons oil in a frying pan and fry the fish cakes on both sides, until they are crisp and golden. Drain on paper towels or a brown paper bag before serving.

What do ghosts have for breakfast?
—Dreaded Wheat!

After carving your pumpkin, save the flesh to make delicious dishes such as pumpkin soup, pumpkin pie, or roasted pumpkin.

CHEESY TOASTS FROM HELL. Grate a scant $\frac{3}{4}$-cup (75 g) hard cheese—Cheddar, Double Gloucester, or Red Leicester—into a bowl and mix well with 2 teaspoons mustard, 2 tablespoons milk, and some salt and pepper. Add a few drops of Worcestershire and Tabasco sauce—as much as you dare! Toast one side of 2 slices of bread under a hot grill, cut off the crusts, and spread the cheese mixture over the untoasted sides. Return to the grill pan and grill until the cheese is golden and bubbly. Serve hot.

Colcannon is a traditional Irish dish. Fry chopped onion in butter and add cooked mashed potato and chopped cabbage or kale. Stir in cream and chopped scallions, and heat until cooked through, stirring frequently. Serve piping hot, with a pat of butter melting on top and in the Irish tradition, a ring buried in it. The person who finds the ring will be married within the year!

Did you ever eat Colcannon
When t'was made with thickened cream
And the greens and scallions blended
Like the picture in a dream?
Did you ever scoop a hole on top
To hold the melting cake
Of clover-flavored butter
That your mother used to make?

(Traditional Irish song)

FORTUNE TELLER'S SOUP. Chop an onion and a rib of celery and cook in a little oil and butter in a saucepan over medium heat for about 10 minutes, until soft. Peel and chop 2 carrots and 2 potatoes and add to the pan. Cook, stirring, for 2 minutes. Add a squirt of tomato purée, then pour in 4 cups (900 ml) chicken or vegetable stock. Increase the heat until the soup starts to boil, then put a lid on the pan, reduce the heat to low and let cook for 30 minutes. Allow the soup to cool, then whizz it up in a blender or food processor until smooth. Return it to the pan and reheat over medium heat. Meanwhile, cook 4 ounces (125 g) alphabet pasta in a pan of boiling salted water for 3 minutes, or according to the instructions on the packet. Drain and add to the soup just before serving. (Serves 4.)

What kind of fruit does a vampire like?
—Neckterines!

BACON SAUSAGES. Slightly stretch 8 streaky pieces of bacon and wrap each one around a sausage. To bake, heat the oven to 400°F (200°C/gas 6), brush a baking sheet with oil, and arrange the bacon-wrapped sausages on the sheet in a single layer. Bake for 20 minutes, turning them over halfway through cooking.

What kind of spirits serve food and drink on airplanes?
—Air ghostesses.

MENACING MEATBALLS. Mix 2 cups, firmly packed (450 g) hamburger or minced pork, or a mixture of the two, with 1 grated onion and 1 beaten egg. Stir in 1 tablespoon dried breadcrumbs and season with salt and pepper. Form the mixture into 24 balls. Pour enough oil into a frying pan to coat the surface and fry the meatballs over medium heat, turning frequently, until they are brown all over. Drain on paper towels. The meatballs can be stirred into hot tomato sauce and served with pasta or speared onto cocktail sticks and served with a dip.

BATS' TOENAIL BREAKFAST
SUNDAE. Combine 3 tablespoons
rolled oats (the bats' toenails!) with
2 tablespoons apple juice and
1 teaspoon liquid honey. Spoon
half the mixture into dessert
glasses and add a layer of
yogurt. Add the rest of the
mixture and another layer of
yogurt on top. A few sliced
almonds on top look like the
toenails of a larger animal.

DEAD BUG PANCAKES. Sift a packed $\frac{1}{4}$-cup (150 g) all-purpose flour with 1 teaspoon baking soda into a mixing bowl. Stir in 2 teaspoons sugar. Add 1 egg and beat with a wooden spoon or whisk, gradually adding in a scant $\frac{3}{4}$-cup (150 ml) milk. Stir in a handful of raisins or golden raisins to look like dead bugs! Place a non-stick frying pan over medium heat and grease it lightly with butter or oil. Drop small tablespoonfuls of batter into the pan; after a minute or so, bubbles will appear and when they start to become small holes, the pancakes can be turned over and cooked for another minute on the other side. Repeat until all the batter has been used up.

BLACK BANANAS. Place unpeeled bananas on a baking sheet and put them in a 400°F (200°C/gas 6) oven for 25 minutes, until the skins have turned black. Slit each one lengthways and push a few chunks of chocolate into the soft banana inside. Sprinkle with brown sugar and add a dollop of cream.

What are a ghost's favorite fruits? —Boonanas and Booberries.

Make a graveyard cake. Cover a square cake with green icing, then make tombstone shapes from smaller pieces of cake. Write on the tombstones using a food-coloring pen.

SPIDER'S WEB DIP. Mix about 4 to 5 tablespoons each of sour cream and mayonnaise and a packet of dry onion soup mix. Put it in a shallow serving bowl and squirt a spiral of green ketchup over the top. With a cocktail stick, draw lines from the center to the rim of the dish to create a spider's web pattern. Serve it with red and green bell pepper "fingers."

MUMMY WRAPS. These make a nice change from ordinary sandwiches. You can buy wraps or flour tortillas from supermarkets. Spread 1 tablespoon mayonnaise over a wrap and add your choice of shredded lettuce, chopped tomatoes, grated cheese, cooked ham or chicken, and drained canned beans such as cannellini, borlotti or red kidney beans. Do not overfill—just keep the ingredients in a neat row across the center. Then roll up as tightly as you can, tucking in the sides

ROASTED PUMPKIN SOUP. Slice a pumpkin into wedges and remove the seeds. Brush the cut surfaces with oil and place in a preheated oven at its hottest setting, 450°F (230°C/gas 8) for 25 minutes. Meanwhile, soften a chopped onion in a little oil, add 4 cups (900 ml) chicken or vegetable stock and 2 cups (450 ml) milk. Bring to boiling point and then simmer gently. When the pumpkin is soft and charred, peel it, cut it into chunks, and add it to the soup. Season with salt, pepper, and nutmeg and cook for about 15 to 20 minutes. Purée and sieve it to remove any fibrous pieces. Serve hot with a dollop of plain yogurt or crème fraîche.

STUFFED PUMPKIN. Cut out a circle around the stem of a small pumpkin and scrape out the seeds and pulp. Place the pumpkin and lid in a baking dish and add about an inch of water. Bake in a 350°F (180°C/gas 4) oven for about 30 minutes, until soft but not collapsed. Fill with cooked rice mixed with corn kernels, peas, grated cheese, cooked chicken or pork—or whatever combination you choose. Place the lid on top and return the stuffed pumpkin to the oven and bake for about 10 to 15 minutes. Bake one pumpkin for each dinner guest. You can vary the fillings according to each person's preferences.

ROASTED PUMPKIN SEEDS. Rinse pumpkin seeds to remove stringy bits of pulp. You will need about 2 cups (230 g) for this recipe. In a medium bowl, combine 1 teaspoon Worcestershire sauce, 3 tablespoons melted butter, and 1 teaspoon salt. Add the seeds and stir until they are all coated. Spread on a baking sheet and bake in a low oven for 1 to 2 hours, until crisp. Stir frequently, to prevent scorching.

PINK SQUIDGE. Boil some water in a kettle. Meanwhile, break up a packet of raspberry gelatin into cubes and place these in a heatproof measuring jug. Pour boiling water into the jug until the liquid reaches the 400-ml mark. Stir until the jelly cubes dissolve, then add cold water to make 600 ml. Leave to cool slightly, then whisk in a scant $\frac{3}{4}$-cup (150 g) plain yogurt. Pour into four serving glasses and sprinkle a layer of mini marshmallows on top of each one. Chill in the refrigerator until set— about 2 to 3 hours. Before serving, top with chocolate sprinkles.

Where do ghosts buy
their food?
—At the ghost-ery store.

GARLIC CATERPILLAR LOAF. Mash 2 tablespoons
butter with a crushed garlic clove and a sprinkling
of dried herbs such as thyme or oregano. Cut
French bread into slices and butter both sides of
each slice with the garlic and herb butter. Wrap in
aluminum foil and bake for 10 minutes at 400°F
(200°C/gas 6). Add two olive eyes and it will look
like a caterpillar. Turn it into a centipede by
spearing stuffed olives on cocktail sticks and
placing these along both sides as legs.

BATTY BROWNIES. Heat the oven to 350°F (180°C/gas 4). Break 9 ounces (250 g) chocolate into pieces and put them, with an equal amount of butter, in a heatproof bowl. Place the bowl in a double boiler and heat on low until the chocolate and butter have melted. Alternatively, melt the chocolate and butter in a microwave. In a separate bowl, beat together 4 eggs, packed 1 cup (250 g) sugar, and a few drops of vanilla extract. Pour the melted chocolate and butter into the egg mixture and whisk until well blended. Add packed 1 cup (125 g) all-purpose flour and a pinch of salt and gently stir into the chocolate mixture, along with 4 ounces (125 g) chocolate (semisweet, milk, or white), chopped into small chunks. Line a 12 x 8-inch (30 x 20 cm) rectangular cake pan with baking parchment. Pour the mixture into the pan and bake for 35 minutes, until the top is crisp and pale. Remove from the oven, let cool for 10 minutes, then transfer the cake onto a wire rack, to finish cooling. Cut into 24 squares. Tell your friends that the chocolate chunks are bat droppings!

What do baby ghosts drink?
—Evaporated milk.

Games
and
Activities

Borrow a camera and take photographs of your friends and family dressed up in Halloween costumes. The pictures will be a great souvenir that you can look back on in years to come.

Borrow a video camera and make your own horror film. Enlist the help of friends and family as "actors."

Make an animated film using dolls and action figures and create your own special effects such as snowstorms, wind, and rain.

Why did the witches' team
lose the baseball game?
—Their bats flew away.

Another way to make an animated film is to use modeling clay, which stays soft so you can bend your molded creatures into different positions.
You can also give them different facial expressions.

Use puppets to put on a show for your family. Finger puppets, glove puppets, and string puppets can all be used.

Very small children can have fun making hand print spiders. Paint all four fingers and the palm of your hand black, using poster paint—but do not paint your thumb. Press your hand on to a sheet of paper, with fingers spread out. Now paint your other hand in the same way and stamp it in the opposite direction, overlapping the palm prints. Buy some wiggly eyes from a craft store and stick them on to your eight-legged spider.

If you don't have special Halloween dolls or puppets, make costumes for the ones you do have. You can dress them as vampires, witches, and werewolves.

Dim the lights and use battery-operated flashlights to illuminate your little characters and create a spooky atmosphere.

Get together with a group of friends to prepare and perform a Halloween play. Your subject could be Dracula, Frankenstein, or another gruesome tale.

Why did the ghost's mail-box rattle?
—It was full of chain letters.

You and two friends could learn some of the witches' speeches from Shakespeare's *Macbeth*.
"Hubble, bubble. Toil and trouble...."

Learn some simple magic tricks and perform them for family and friends. If you know other people who can do tricks, you could have a Halloween magic contest.

Using a desk lamp pointed at a blank wall or large sheet of paper, have a go at making spooky shadows with your hands—try a ghost, a werewolf, a bat, then see what others you can do.

Tell a spooky story, adding sound effects as you go. Wobble a large sheet of cardboard or a metal oven tray to make the sound of thunder, flap a plastic bag to make the sound of bats flying, pour uncooked rice onto a baking sheet to sound like rain. It's even better if you can borrow a microphone because it will amplify spooky whispers and groans. You could enlist the help of a friend so that you can concentrate on the storytelling while he or she supplies the appropriate sounds.

Be a Halloween stand-up. It's not just a matter of standing there and telling a few jokes. Make sure you know some real side-splitters and practice them a few times—you don't want to forget any punchlines in the middle of your routine!

Organize a guided tour of an imaginary castle or laboratory. Blindfold your victim and escort him or her on a tactile tour of your house. You will need to do some preparation, such as setting up an air conditioner behind a door, corn flakes that crunch underfoot in a passageway, a sound system with a cassette or CD of eerie sounds in an upstairs bedroom, a dripping tap in the bathroom, and strands of thread hanging from door frames.

Use an upturned bowl or a pearly white balloon as a crystal ball, dress up as a gypsy, and tell everyone's fortune.

What do ghouls send home when they're on holiday? —Ghostcards.

Make a set of cards for telling fortunes. On each small piece of card, write a prediction. Dress up as a gypsy, a witch, or a magician. Spread out the cards and ask your "victim" to choose one, then read the prediction in a dark and mysterious voice.

Make a Fortune Spinner. Draw three concentric circles on a piece of cardboard and cut it out around the outer circle. Divide the circle into 12 segments. You will now have 36 separate boxes in which to write predictions! Make a spinner with an arrow shape cut from card with a pin stuck through into a piece of cork. Stand it in the center of the circle. Spin the arrow and when it stops, read the prediction on the appropriate section. Predictions can be just one or two words. Before you spin the arrow, ask a question such as "Will I pass my exams?" to which the reply might be, "Seek help." How you interpret the answer is up to you—you are the fortune teller!

Or fill a notebook with "answers" and vague predictions, one to a page. Ask a question and then open the book at random to read your reply. Predictions could be: you will achieve success, you will need assistance, don't be afraid, follow your heart, think again, trust your instincts, and so on.

Pretend you are an astrologer. Ask your friends what their star signs are and make predictions for the coming week, month, or year.

Rent or borrow a scary video. You could turn out all the lights to add to the fear factor—but don't invite anyone who frightens very easily and check the rating of anything you show.

What did the ghost install on his computer?
—A scream saver!

Enjoy the season. Go for a walk in your neighborhood and see what decorations everyone else has put up. You could even take some photographs. Halloween doesn't last long, so make the most of it.

Try blow-painting with a straw and some paint. Dribble runny paint onto a piece of paper and blow through a straw to make spidery patterns.

Create a random pattern that looks like a
spider's web. Cut a round piece of black
paper to fit into the bottom of a cake tin.
Drip a teaspoonful of white paint on to
the middle of the paper, then place a
marble in the paint. Tilt the cake tin back
and forth and the marble will leave trails
of white paint on the paper.

To make a spider's web picture, mix equal parts of flour, salt, and water in a large bowl. Pour the mixture into an empty liquid detergent bottle. Squeeze this "3D paint" onto black paper and, while it's still wet, sprinkle it with glitter. When it dries, you can hang this spider's web picture on the wall.

Another good technique for Halloween pictures is to draw your basic design on white paper with a white candle. Brush watercolor or poster paint over it—the paint will cover the paper but not the areas of candle wax. Try drawing a spider's web, a ghost, or any kind of seasonal picture.

To create a scratchy picture, cover a sheet of paper with patches of color, using colored pencils or wax crayons. Then cover the whole thing with a thick layer of black wax crayon. Scratch a design into the black layer to reveal the colors beneath.

Buy or borrow an assortment of Halloween cookie cutters. Dip each one into paint and then press onto paper. You can fill in the shapes with a paintbrush. Print shapes onto tissue paper for Halloween gift wrap or print them on sturdier paper and cut out each shape when the paint is dry.

Play with clay. There are different kinds of modeling clay available from craft stores and toy stores. Play-Doh can be molded and re-molded and is very pliable. Squidge it in your hands to create ghosts, ghouls, and monsters.

What do you call a skeleton's bike? —A bone-shaker.

If you have some self-hardening clay, your models can be more permanent. Make crazy Halloween creatures and put them on display. Put them away and get them out again next year.

Create a collage of pictures cut from magazines and newspapers. Look for pictures on a Halloween theme—gravestones, a night sky with a full moon, bats, wolves—or cut out features such as eyes, noses, mouths, and ears, and rearrange them to make scary faces.

Make a Halloween scrapbook.
Include newspaper clippings and
pictures from magazines.

**Make a Halloween newsletter. Use a computer
with a desktop publishing program, if you have
access to one, and print the number of copies you
need. Or do it by hand, sticking down words and
pictures on paper and photocopying the finished
result. Include news about Halloween parties and
other events in your area, ideas for party food or
costumes, jokes, and stories—whatever you like.**

Make a spooky calendar to count down the days to Halloween—like a Christmas advent calendar. You will need two sheets of cardstock or heavy paper. Make square windows in the top piece by cutting around three sides of each one so you can fold it back. And draw scary pictures or write little messages on the other piece that will show if you open the window above it on the top piece.

Organize a Halloween party or sleepover. Plan ahead by making a list of all the things you plan to do and all the people you want to invite. Send out invitations a few weeks ahead of time and begin preparing some of the food a few days in advance.

If you have been invited to a Halloween party, get organized. Plan what you are going to wear and what you need to take.

Send out Halloween greetings. It's a great time of year to keep in touch with family and friends, so send them a card or an e-mail.

Send a friend a spooky greetings card. For a really simple design, cut a skull and crossbones from white paper and stick onto a folded sheet of heavy black paper.

For a more intricate greeting card, cut out an outline of a spooky landscape, complete with a haunted castle, from black paper and glue it onto a folded piece of heavy orange paper. Cut out a white paper moon, a little white ghost, and black bats to add to the card.

If you are having a party or a few friends over at Halloween, make invitation cards. Cut a pumpkin head shape from orange paper, complete with cut-out eyes and mouth, and glue it onto a yellow piece of paper. Cut around it again—the yellow paper looks like a light shining out through the eyes and mouth. Make lots of these—they are quick and easy to do—and stick them to rectangles of card. Add greetings you have made on the computer or stick on letters to spell out the word "party" on the front.

Make Halloween potato prints.
Cut a potato in half and use a sharp knife to carve your design on the cut surface (with adult help).
Try cutting a pumpkin face, a bat, a cat, a moon, or a skull and crossbones—it's up to you.
Use poster paints to print on paper or fabric paints to print on fabric.

You could also try pumpkin printing. Cut pumpkin flesh into pieces and dip them into paint to make prints.

Host a Halloween treasure hunt. Hollow out a pumpkin, fill it with goodies, and hide it. Write clues on cutout paper bones, or make a spooky-looking map to lead your guests to the prize.

Create a pumpkin puzzle. Scoop out the seeds and flesh from two medium-sized pumpkins, then cut each one into a dozen pieces. Split players into two teams and give each group a supply of toothpicks and the pieces of one of the pumpkins. The object of the game is to reassemble the pumpkin using toothpicks to hold the pieces together.

Make a Halloween stencil. Cut a simple shape from the center of a piece of stiff cardboard. Lay this stencil on a piece of paper and use a sponge or a stubby brush to dab thick paint through the holes. Carefully lift the stencil to reveal your design.

Halloween stencils can be used to decorate all kinds of things, such as wrapping paper and invitation cards. And if you use fabric paint, you can stencil onto tablecloths, pillow cases, T-shirts, and other fabric items.

Using a pen and ink and some kitchen parchment paper, create a spooky scroll. Look in the library for a book on calligraphy and try copying some ancient lettering. When you have practiced enough, write a ghostly poem or the last will and testament of some imaginary character. Crumple the paper, tear the edges, and rub it with some earth to make it look old and worn, then roll it up and tie it with a torn strip of fabric.

Make a Halloween handkerchief using fabric paints and pens. On a plain white handkerchief, paint a few bright blobs. Add eight legs to each to turn them into spiders, then draw a web with a black fabric pen.

Use large sheets of paper and chunky wax crayons or dark pastel chalks to take rubbings from tombs in your local church or graveyard. You may have to ask permission first. Tape the paper onto the gravestone and then rub your crayon or chalk over the paper, pressing hard enough so that the lettering appears on the paper.

Make a Halloween treasure map. Once again, try to make it look like an antique. Draw your map on thick white or cream paper, using pencils, felt tip pens, or inks, then dip a rag in some beeswax furniture polish and rub it in. It will make the paper look a bit like parchment.

Why did the headless horseman go into business?
—He wanted to get a-head.

Visit an art gallery and go on a treasure hunt, looking for scary details in the paintings and sculptures on display. Use the details you discover in your own works of art.

Make walnut spiders. Take half a walnut shell and leave it natural or paint it black. Attach pipe cleaners to the sides of the shell, using glue or tape, and stick on googly eyes.

Make beastly beads from self-hardening clay. Roll small lumps of clay into balls and pierce them with a thin stick to create a hole for threading. These are the beastly bodies. Then add details such as wings, heads, and legs with more clay but make sure they are not too delicate. Let the clay dry and then paint your beastly beads. After the paint has dried, spray clear glossy paint onto them for a shiny surface. Thread them onto a necklace.

Where did the ghost throw the soccer ball?
—Over the ghoul line.

Make a ghost necklace by pouring a small, ghost-shaped puddle of white glue onto a small square of waxed paper and let it dry for two or three days. Peel it off the paper and use a hole punch to make a hole near the top. Add eyes and mouth to your ghost using a black marker pen. Cut some pretty string or yarn long enough to make a necklace and thread the ghost through the hole.

Make a hanging ghost from a white balloon and two white plastic bags from the store. Cut the handles off the bags and cut them into strips, starting at the top edge and stopping about 2 inches (5 cm) from the base. Tape this plastic fringe around the top end of the inflated balloon. Using a black marker pen, draw two eyes and a mouth on the balloon. Tie string to the knotted end and hang it up.

Where do baby ghosts go during the day?
—To a day-scare center.

To make a cheesecloth ghost, first blow up a small balloon and put it in a bowl to steady it while you work. Cut two 12-inch (30 cm) squares of cheesecloth or muslin. Dilute white glue with an equal amount of water, dip the fabric in the mixture, and wring out the excess. Drape the fabric over the balloon to form a ghostly shape. Let it dry overnight, then remove the balloon and glue on googly eyes. Attach a length of nylon thread to the top if you want to hang it up, or you can simply stand it on a table or shelf.

What's a ghost's favorite ride at the funfair?
—The roller ghoster.

To make stained glass pictures to decorate a window, cut large shapes from black paper—a bat, a cat, a pumpkin head, a ghost, or a witch—and cut out big, round eyes. Glue colored tissue paper scraps over the eyeholes, then tape the shapes to a window so the light shines through the tissue.

Make spider cups to use for party drinks or fill with candy by cutting four pipe cleaners in half to make eight legs. Fold over one end of each pipe cleaner by about $\frac{1}{4}$ inch (5 mm). Glue or tape the folded part to the side of the cup, placing four legs on each side, then glue googly eyes to the front of the cup.

Make a spider puppet from a paper plate with pipe cleaner legs and googly eyes. Punch two holes in the plate and thread a string through each hole. By holding one string in each hand, you can make the spider "walk."

FRIGHTFUL FINGER PUPPETS.
Cut a finger off an old glove and stitch or glue pieces of felt or other heavy fabric onto the glove finger to make Halloween characters such as a bug, a vampire, or a witch.

You can also make finger puppets from paper. Draw the top half of a Halloween character such as Frankenstein's monster. At the base of the body, cut out two finger holes and push your fingers through to the front, to act as legs. You could wear gloves or cover your fingers with makeup to match the puppet's outfit.

Make a bat from a wire coat hanger and a black plastic garbage bag. Bend the coat hanger to resemble bat wings. Lay the plastic garbage bag on a flat surface and place the hanger on top. Using black electrical tape, tape the hanger to the bag, and trim off any excess close to the wire. Cut a 16-inch (40 cm) circle of black plastic for the head. Crumple newspaper into a ball and tape the circle over it, then tape it to the hook of the coat hanger. Make a body from crumpled black plastic and tape this in the center of the wings. Cut eyes and fangs from white paper or reflective tape and glue them on.

Make a collection bucket. Cover a giant waxed paper cup—the kind you get full of popcorn at the movies or a soft drink at a concession stand—with several layers of papier mâché to strengthen it and give a good surface for painting. Let it dry before painting the outside black and the inside a contrasting color. When the paint is dry, decorate with a spider's web, using a glitter glue stick.

Make a more sturdy trick-or-treat bag from fabric, even if your sewing skills are pretty basic. Fleece and felt do not fray and are easy to stitch. Cut two pieces of fleece (you could use an old sweatshirt), 10 x 8 inches (25 x 20 cm) in size. Cut a bold Halloween figure from felt—a spooky pumpkin face from orange and green or maybe just a pair of staring eyes from white and black. Stitch your design in place on one of the pieces of fleece and put the two "wrong sides" of the pieces of fleece together—the design will be on the inside. Stitch together the sides and the bottom, about $\frac{1}{2}$ inch (1 cm) from the edges. Turn $\frac{3}{4}$ inch (2 cm) under on the top edge to form a hem and stitch down the hem. Sew pieces of cord to the top of the bag for handles.

Transform a sturdy brown paper bag with a handle into a trick-or-treat bag. Draw a pumpkin face, a black cat, or other Halloween face on the front. Cut ears out of paper and stick onto each side. Cut away the eyes, tape colored cellophane candy wrappers over the holes, and put a small flashlight inside the bag.

You can also make a great trick-or-treat bag from an old pair of jeans. Cut the legs off the jeans, leaving the top part to make your bag. Turn it inside out and stitch the cut edges together to form the base of the bag. Cut a 2-inch (5 cm) wide strip from the inside leg seam of each leg to form a strap. Stitch each end of the strap to the bag.

HALLOWEEN CONFETTI. Punch out shapes from sheets of black, orange, and green paper, using a regular hole punch or one of the fancy ones you can find at craft stores that punch out little shapes—stars, for example. Sprinkle it on your "victims" as you mumble an ancient curse. You can also scatter it over a party table.

What kind of music do mummies listen to?
—Wrap!

Use scissors with wiggly blades to cut thin, short strips of colored paper and mix this with your punched-out confetti.

Make a treat jar from a clean empty jelly or pickle jar. Decorate the jar by painting it with special glass paints—what about a graveyard scene silhouetted in black with a silver moon and stars? Make a handle by winding pipe cleaners around the neck of the jar.

A few days before Halloween, make up treat bags for anyone coming to your house.

Make Halloween crackers. Cut a rectangle of black crepe paper, making sure the ridges in the paper run along the length of the rectangle. Place a cardboard tube that's shorter than the paper in the center of it. Roll the paper around the tube and glue in place. Tie one end closed. Write a Halloween greeting on a slip of paper and put it in the tube, along with a wrapped piece of candy or a small seasonal gift, then tie the other end closed. Make lots of crackers in this way and decorate the outside of each one with paper cutouts.

Why is a vampire like a computer? —They both have mega-bites.

Try sticking fake gems onto glass. Use white glue or a hot glue gun (with adult supervision). Combine glass paints and fake gems for really dazzling effects. What about painting a black cat and gluing fake emeralds onto it for eyes?

Make gnarled faces from dried apples. Peel a large apple and coat it with a mixture of lemon juice and salt to prevent browning. Use a potato peeler or small knife to carve out eye sockets, a nose, mouth, and ears. Don't bother with smaller details because they won't show after the apple is dry. Insert whole cloves for eyes and raw rice grains for teeth. Place apples on a wire rack in a warm, dry place for about two weeks or speed up the drying process a little by placing in an oven set at the lowest temperature for several days.

HALLOWEEN PENCIL TOPPERS.

Stick the blunt end of a pencil or pen into a small lump of self-hardening clay. Then mold the clay into a ghost or a monster. You could mold a whole creature or just its head. Let it dry, then paint your pencil topper to make it look really gruesome.

Play a ghostly party game—this is not for the faint-hearted! Fill plastic containers such as clean, empty margarine tubs. Put peeled grapes in one, cooked spaghetti in another, cold, cooked rice in another, and an apple with holes cut out for mouth, nose and eyes in one. A group of friends should sit in a circle, blindfolded, while you tell them a scary story. As you recount the gruesome details, pass around the bowls, encouraging them to feel the contents. When you mention maggots, pass the bowl of rice around; as you mention eyeballs, pass around the grapes. The cooked spaghetti feels like guts and the apple, a shrunken head. Make up your own stories depending on what you have available. Don't stop at the list above, try using things such as clean chicken bones for human bones, pumpkin seeds for bats' toenails, and dental floss for goblin's hair. Let your imagination run wild!

How many words can you make from the word "Halloween?" Play the game on your own or, if you have friends around, play it in pairs. Give everyone paper and pencil and set a time limit. Whoever comes up with the most words is the winner.

What is a witch's favorite subject at school? —Spelling.

Play a Halloween memory game. Put some items on a tray—a pumpkin, a pair of plastic fangs, an apple, a toy bat, a fake eyeball, and so on—and let players look at it for a minute. Then cover it up and see how many items people can remember. The person who writes down all the items—or most of them—wins a prize.

Play Halloween Bingo. To make bingo cards, collect suitable pictures—various scary characters, symbols and animals associated with Halloween—and make photocopies. Each card should have the same number of pictures but a different combination of them. You will also need to put a set of single pictures in a bowl that correspond to the pictures on the cards. Pull these pictures out of the bowl, one by one, and call out a description. Each person who has a picture of that item on his or her card can cover it up with a bottle top or a piece of blank card. The first to cover up all their pictures—or maybe even the first five pictures—is the winner.

Why not whip up a worm pie? Place some sweet gummy worms in a baking dish and squirt a thick layer of whipped cream from an aerosol can on top. Throw a dice to determine the order of play. Players can be blindfolded and they have to retrieve worms from the cream, using their teeth—no hands! You may want to provide a bib to protect clothing because this game can be very messy.

For another messy party game, fill a large plastic bowl or bucket with over-cooked spaghetti or jelly or something equally slurpy. Bury wrapped candies and other washable treats deep inside. Players should be blindfolded before they plunge their hands, elbow-deep, into the gunk in order to retrieve one of the treats.

Play "scabs." Place wrapped candies in a large dish and fill the dish with cornflakes to represent scabs. Tie the players' hands behind their backs and let them retrieve one of the candies using only their teeth!

Play vampire-race. Fill small bowls with equal amounts of tomato juice to represent blood. Give each player a plastic teaspoon and on the word "go," they have to drink the juice using the spoons. The fastest wins!

What is a vampire's favorite sport? —Casketball.

Play bony fingers. Scatter nuts or small candies on the table or on a large sheet of paper or plastic on the floor. Each player has to try to pick up the nuts or candies using chopsticks—bony fingers. You could set a time limit, with the person who picks up the most in, say, two minutes, as the winner!

Why didn't the skeleton want to do a parachute jump?
—He didn't have the guts.

Monster hands. Sit in a circle on the floor around a plate or chopping board with a huge chocolate bar on it, a knife and fork, and pair of thick gardening gloves. Roll two dice. The first to throw a double six puts on the gloves and attempts to cut off a chunk of chocolate. That player eats the chocolate, using the knife and fork to cut off pieces, until someone else throws a double six, at which point that person takes over. Keep playing until all the chocolate has been eaten!

Play vampire kiss chase.
A variation on a classic playground game, the person who is "the vampire" chases the others and when he or she catches them, pretends to bite them on the neck instead of kissing them. Bitten victims then become vampires, too, and chase the others until everyone has become a vampire.

How can you tell that a vampire likes cricket?
—Every night, he turns into a bat.

Play pass the pumpkin, a variation of pass the parcel. Hollow out a small pumpkin and fill it with candies. Play some music, sit in a circle, and pass the pumpkin around. When the music stops, the person who is holding it takes a candy. The game continues until all the candies are gone.

What type of witch plays cricket? —A wicket witch.

Line up in teams and give the first person in each team an apple to place under his or her chin. The object of the game is to pass the apple to the next in line without using hands. The first team to get it all the way to the last person in the line is the winner. If anyone drops the apple, the team has to start again with the first person in the line.

Try a variation on "pin the tail on the donkey" by drawing a picture of a Halloween character on a large piece of poster paper or board. Hang it on the wall and let blindfolded players try to stick the missing piece on the picture. The one who places it nearest the correct position is the winner. It could be a tail on a devil or witch's cat, a gruesome grin on a pumpkin head, a bolt through Frankenstein's neck, or a gnarled nose on a witch—the choice is yours.

Mummy wrap is a game for small teams of two or three people. Each team has a roll of toilet paper and the idea is to wrap one member of the team to look like a mummy. Once wrapped, the mummy must walk to the other end of the room and back, and then be unwrapped. This could be the end of the game, with the first team to complete the task winning. Or you could extend the game by another member of the same team being wrapped up using the same toilet paper—which means some careful unwrapping first time around, so the paper doesn't get torn!

Another apple game involves tying string to the stem of each apple and suspending a group of them from a beam, a door frame, or a washing line. With hands behind their backs, players must attempt to eat one of the suspended apples. Instead of apples, you could suspend pretzels, marshmallows, or other edible treats.

Bobbing for apples is an ancient game. Simply fill a large container with water and add as many apples as you like— the apples will float. The object of the game is to grab one of the apples and remove it from the water using only your mouth—no hands! Remove the stems from the apples to make it more difficult—and prepare to get wet!

Why don't angry witches ride their brooms?
—They're afraid of flying off the handle.

Organize a peanut race. Give each participant a drinking straw and a peanut. The aim of the game is to hold the straw in your teeth and use it to push and roll the peanut along the ground from the start line to the finish.

While you have drinking straws and peanuts handy, play a gathering game. Give each player a drinking straw and a paper cup and place peanuts in a pile. Each player sucks through the straw to pick up a peanut from the pile and transfer it into the cup. Set a time limit. The winner is the one with the most peanuts in his or her cup when the time is up.

Have a balloon relay race. Divide into teams with one balloon for each team. The first player in each team must cross the room to the other side, then back again, keeping the balloon in the air. Pass the balloon to the next player, who repeats the challenge.

Float some flying bats. Cut large bat shapes from black tissue paper. Give each player a straw. The aim is to keep the bat afloat by blowing through the straw. Or try passing a bat from person to person by sucking on the straw to hold it on the other end and exhaling to let it go.

Have a cookie-decorating competition. Supply plain cookies—or cupcakes—and tubes of icing, with a variety of small candies and cake decorations. Everyone can decorate one or more cookies and you can award prizes for the funniest, the scariest, the best use of icing, or the most decorations on a single cookie!

Decorate plastic or cardboard half masks (available from party stores). Each player gets a plain mask and you can provide stickers, feathers, paper scraps, fake gems, and glue. Not only are the masks fun to make, they are also fun to wear!

Why don't mummies take vacations? —They're afraid they'll relax and unwind.

Have fun with makeup. Do your own face or a friend's, adding a bit of glamour or fantasy to create a great disguise or a complete transformation! Get together as many materials as possible and ask your guests to bring things, too—such as lipsticks, lip and eye pencils, lip gloss, eye shadows, face paints, body glitter, stick-on jewels, and sequins. Makeup brushes, small sponges and cotton wool are also useful. Remember to wipe off the lipsticks and any pencils between users for sanitation's sake.

What is a baby ghost's favorite game?
—Peekaboo.

**Start a group ghost story.
Sitting in a circle, with the lights dimmed, one person starts and speaks for one minute. The person sitting to the right takes over after the first minute. Each person adds to the story until it reaches a scary conclusion.**

FLASHLIGHT TALES. Turn off the lights. Hand a flashlight around and let the person who is holding it be the storyteller. He or she could tell a whole spooky story or just a section before passing on the flashlight to another person.

WINK MURDER. Hand each player a piece of paper. All the pieces are blank, except for one. That one says, "murderer." Everyone sits in a circle without saying anything. The murderer has to wink at each of the other people without getting caught. Anyone who is winked at has to act dead. The remaining players have to guess who the murderer is before he or she can wink at them.

SCARECROW CHALLENGE. Divide into teams. Each team gets a selection of old clothes—a shirt, jeans, belt, straw hat, gloves, and boots. Ask each team to nominate one person to be the scarecrow. The rest of the team has to dress the scarecrow, who should stand on the far side of the room. Each person can then run over in turn, to add an item of clothing to the scarecrow. Or teams could throw a dice, with each number representing a different piece of clothing. The first team to finish dressing their scarecrow is the winner.

PUMPKIN TIDDLEYWINKS. Hollow out a pumpkin and use it as a target. Flip tiddleywinks and see if you can get one inside. Or sit a few yards away and throw ping pong balls, trying to get each one in the pumpkin.

What instrument do skeletons play?
—The trom-bone.

HOLLOW-EEN. Make a Halloween piñata—a big, hollow papier mâché model of a big black cat, a monster's head, or a giant pumpkin. Fill it with candies and treats, suspend it from a tree branch, and let everyone hit it until the treats spill out, in traditional piñata style.

Where do mummies go swimming?
—In the Dead Sea.

BOOGIE MAN BOWLING. Make bowling pins from empty plastic bottles with a little sand or water in each to give them a bit of weight. Decorate by painting with acrylic paints or covering with paper, adding ghoulish faces. Arrange at the end of a path and roll a ball to see how many you can knock down.

Hold a witch hunt. Dress up a doll in a witch's costume. If you don't have the appropriate dolls' clothes, drape black fabric over the toy instead and add a hat made from a black paper cone. Hide it somewhere in the house or garden and let people hunt for it, individually or in teams. The winner—the person who finds the witch— can receive a reward.

Instead of just one witch, you could hunt for dozens of witches. Cut out little witch shapes from black paper and hide them all over the place. The winner is the person who finds the most.

Play "musical graves."

Lay large rectangles of paper on the floor. Then play a variation of musical chairs. Have one fewer grave than there are people playing the game, play some music, and ask everyone to walk around the room like zombies. When the music stops, each person tries to lie down on a grave. The person who fails to find a grave is out and the game continues after one grave has been removed. The game finishes with two people competing for a single grave.

What song does Dracula hate?
—"You Are My Sunshine."

UNTANGLING THE WEB. Cut one long length of string for each pair of players and wind some colored electrical tape around either end of the pieces. In a large room or the yard, lay the pieces out so they resemble a giant spider's web, weaving them in and out of each other. Every player should grab a taped end of a piece of string and start to roll it up into a ball. As they do so, they will have to untie knots and tangles. When the first pair meets in the middle of their piece of string, they are the winners.

A variation of the spider's web game is to attach a prize at the end of the string rather than a person. If you do this, attach the prize with strong tape so it doesn't come off by accident.

JACK BY NUMBERS. This is a variation on an old pencil-and-paper game called "Beetle." Players throw a dice and have to get a certain number to draw a part of a jack-o'-lantern face: 1 for the basic pumpkin shape, 2 for the stem, 3 and 4 for eyes, 5 for a nose and 6 for a mouth. Each item must be drawn in order. If you do not throw the number you need, you must pass the dice to the next player. The aim of the game is to complete a drawing of a jack-o'-lantern before the other players. You can play this in teams or as individuals.

GUESSING GAME. Fill a large glass jar with candies and ask players to guess how many there are. The one whose guess is most accurate is the winner. Fill the jar with special Halloween novelty candies such as gummy worms and candy fingers and eyeballs. It's best to count the candies before you begin and put the paper with the number on it away until the time comes to play the game.

What song did the skeleton sing while he was riding his motorcycle?
—Bone to be wild!

Guess the weight of the pumpkin. Each player can hold the pumpkin—choose a nice big one—and make a guess. After they have all guessed, weigh the pumpkin on the bathroom scales. The one who guessed nearest to the correct weight gets a prize.

HALLOWEEN CHARADES. Cut out small pieces of heavy paper and write the name of a character, a book title, a film, or a song that can be associated with Halloween on each. Players take a card at random and, without showing it to other players, have to act out what's written on the card without speaking. The other players guess.

HALLOWEEN CAPERS. Get everyone to form a line, like a crocodile, and start marching down the street. The leader shouts out instructions such as "fly like a bat" or "creep like a cat" or "float like a ghost" and everyone has to obey.

CREEPY CASTLE MEMORY GAME. The first player starts by saying something like, "I went to the creepy castle and I saw a wicked witch." The next person repeats this and adds something else: "I went to the creepy castle and I saw a wicked witch and an ugly troll." Continue like this until there are too many things to remember.

MELT THE WICKED WITCH. Draw a picture of an evil witch on a blackboard. Provide players with a bucket of water and some sponges and let them take turns throwing wet sponges at the witch until she disappears.

Or ask for a willing volunteer to dress up as a witch and have wet sponges thrown at him or her.

Play a ghostly guessing game. Blindfold one person and stand around him or her, in a circle. Spin that person round and, when he or she stops, the person they face should say, "Whooooooo. Whoooo am I?" The blindfolded person must guess and, if correct, the blindfold passes to the person he or she guessed and the game continues.

Where do ghosts water ski? —On Lake Erie.

Fill the sugar bowl with salt and wait and see what happens when everyone sprinkles it on their cereal or in their tea or coffee.

Put ice cubes with a plastic fly frozen into them in your parents' drinks.

Wake up your brother or sister at 7 o'clock on Saturday morning and tell them they are late for school!

Empty the shampoo bottle and fill it with honey!

Soak everyone's toothbrushes (apart from your own!) in lemon juice or vinegar, or sprinkle with garlic powder for a nasty morning-time shock!

Put fake bugs in your parents' bed.

Tie some tin cans to the rear bumper of your parents' car.

Use superglue to stick a coin to the sidewalk, then hide until someone tries to pick it up— jump out shouting, "Trick-or-treat!"

Put a rubber snake in your mother's underwear drawer.

Replace your dad's can of shaving cream with a can of whipped cream.

When your dad is asleep, squirt some shaving cream into the palm of his hand, then tickle his nose with a feather and see what happens when he goes to itch.

Draw frightful faces on your breakfast hard-cooked eggs—or on all the eggs in the fridge.

Buy some blood capsules from your local joke store—bite into them at an appropriate moment to give your friends or relatives a nasty shock.

Devise some fiendish tricks to play on willing victims as you go out and about on All Hallows' Eve. And don't forget to carry a bucket or bag in which to collect all your booty.

Fake a severed finger. Cut a hole in the base of a small plastic container and put a cotton wool ball in the bottom. Stick your middle finger through the hole, gripping the container with the rest of your fingers. Drip red paint or ketchup on the cotton wool around your finger. Cover the container and ask your unsuspecting victim to remove the lid—then wiggle your finger!

TRICK-OR-TREAT LUCKY DIP. Place slips of paper in a bucket and on each one write a different trick or forfeit, such as "howl like a wolf" or "screech like a banshee." Ask your victim to select a piece of paper at random, and you will agree to do what it says. That should be worth a Halloween sticker or a bag of candies!

MYSTERY BOX. Paint a cardboard shoebox black and cut a hole in the lid. Place something "sinister" in the box and invite people to put their hand in and guess what it is.

Collect lots of brochures and pamphlets in the weeks leading up to Halloween. Mail these to your victim or shove them under his or her door. Offer to put an end to the junk mail barrage in return for a treat.

Push cotton wool balls through your victim's mailbox and shout "It's snowing!"

If you know your neighbors well, scratch at their doors (without damaging the paintwork!) and howl like a wolf.

Coat the palm of your hand with something slimy and shake hands with everyone you meet. Hair gel is quite effective.

Mix flour, toothpaste, and shampoo in a large bowl, add plastic bugs, and dare people to put their hand in.

Fill a bottle with nasty smells! Mix vinegar, garlic, shampoo, all sorts of weird and wonderful ingredients, until you have produced a stinky potion. Make a label for the bottle with a skull and crossbones and the word "poison." Keep the bottle corked until your "victim" is ready to smell it. (And use a plastic bottle, not a glass one, for safety.)

Carry a cookie tin and a wooden spoon and rattle the spoon in the tin, making as much noise as you can, promising to stop if and when you are offered a treat.

March up and down the street, banging a drum or blowing a trumpet, and shouting "Happy Halloween!"

Carry a tape or CD player with you, with a pre-recorded tape or disc of spooky noises. You can buy a special sound effects recording from a record store, or make your own. Place the speaker near the open mailbox or a window and turn up the volume.

At the end of the evening, you may want to keep all your ill-gotten gains for yourself—or you may decide to pool all your treats with friends or siblings and share them out equally.

Don't forget the grown-ups! They've helped you with your costumes, fixed your makeup, and accompanied you on your tour of the neighborhood—don't they deserve a candy or a chocolate bar?

If you're out and about, trick-or-treating, this Halloween, follow a few basic safety rules.

Children under 12 should be accompanied by an adult.

Children should travel only in familiar areas and along an established route.

Draw a map of the area for children to carry with them, with the houses to visit clearly marked. This will help them to find their way around safely.

Plan and discuss your intended route with parents and make sure they know the names of your companions.

Perhaps you could arrange a parents' relay, with one parent starting out as chaperone and handing over to another along the route.

Children should knock only at houses that are well-lit and should never enter a stranger's home.

It is a good idea for children to carry some change for a phone call in case they encounter a problem.

Agree on a time for children to return home from trick-or-treating and make sure they are carrying a watch so that they know what time it is.

Wait until you get home before eating any of the candies you have been given—and make sure an adult inspects your ill-gotten gains.

Be safe if you have to cross any streets.

Children may encounter naked flames—candles and jack-o'-lanterns—so make sure costumes are fire retardant.

Wear warm clothes if you are going out on a cold evening. If your costume is skimpy, wear a coat over it or some warm underwear underneath.

If your child's costume is very elaborate, make sure that they are wearing more simple clothing underneath so that, if necessary, they can change to play games, or take a break.

Avoid all-in-one, single-piece costumes that don't allow for easy movement, proper air circulation, or going to the bathroom in a hurry!

If your costume is long, make sure it's not a tripping hazard—you don't want to fall and hurt yourself— you'd miss all the fun!

Make sure your child's costume is fairly sturdy—you don't want it to fall to pieces before the end of the evening.

If you are wearing a costume of dark-colored materials on a dark night, add a few strips of reflective tape on both the front and back.

Give your child some glow sticks to carry—available from camping stores.

For youngsters under the age of 12, attach a card with their names, addresses, and telephone numbers (including their area code) to their clothes where it will be easy to find in an emergency.

If you are wearing a mask, make sure it doesn't obscure your vision—and make sure it has nose and mouth openings as well as large eye holes.

You could use face paints instead of a mask if you are worried about impairing your child's vision.

Any knives, swords or other accessories that are part of your costume should be made of cardboard or flexible plastic. It is dangerous to carry sharp objects.

Carry a battery-operated flashlight to help you find your way on dark pathways. It will also allow you to be seen more clearly by other people.

Walk from house to house—don't run. And be careful when crossing lawns and grassy areas where the ground may be uneven.

Walk on the pavement, not in the road, even on the quietest street.

If there are no pavements, walk on the side of the road facing the traffic.

Some parents just don't like the idea of their kids going out at night to trick-or-treat. If you want your children to stay in, at least try to make it fun for them by organizing some Halloween fun and games.

Halloween
for
Grown-ups

October 31, the "night of the dead," is remembered and observed in many cultures. You could observe a few ancient customs or rituals yourself—dress up, play a few tricks, or throw a wild Halloween party. It's up to you!

Don't let the children have all the fun this year. Be sure to join in and have some Halloween fun of your own!

Trick-or-treat, Trick-or-treat,
Give me something nice to eat,
If you don't dare, I don't care,
I'll put a spider in your underwear.

What do you get when you cross a vampire and a snowman?
—Frostbite.

What do you get if you cross Dracula with Al Capone?
—A fangster.

Follow the age-old ritual of leaving out food for the dead or cook a special meal that your own dearly departed once enjoyed.

What did the big ghost say to
the little ghost?
—Don't spook until you're spooken to!

**Watch *The Rocky Horror Picture Show* on video
or DVD. Dress up as your favorite character and
sing along with the songs.**

What kind of dog does Dracula have?
—A bloodhound.

**Fill the bathroom with candles and run a bath full
of bubbles. It will create a magical atmosphere
and put you in the mood for the antics of the
evening ahead.**

What do ghosts use to wash their hair?
—Sham-boo.

What do you call two spiders that just got married?
—Newlywebs.

Hold a séance. Get together with a group of friends and try to get in touch with "the other side."

Go trick-or-treating. Knock on your neighbor's door and then hide. You could also push a rubber bat through their mailbox.

Fill your pockets with candies in case you meet some Halloween pranksters when you are out and about.

What is Transylvania?
—Dracula's terror-tory.

What do you call a war between groups of vampires?
—A bat-tle.

Break the rules. If your children are not normally allowed sweet treats, let them have a few, just for one night.

Extend the curfew. Everyone will be staying up a bit later on Halloween. Make bedtime a little later, for once.

How do you greet Her Majesty on October 31?
—"Hallo Queen!"

Volunteer your services as a face painter, if you are skilled in that area. Let your children invite a few friends over and do their makeup for them.

Let trick-or-treaters know that they are welcome by putting up a sign saying so!

Did you hear about the twin witches?
—No one could tell which witch was which!

Decorate the outside of your house with pumpkin lanterns, banners, and wreaths.

Let everyone know that they can make your house the last stop on their trick-or-treat rounds and make them welcome with a hot drink and something good to eat.

What happened when two vampires liked each other?
—It was love at first bite!

Hard-cook the smallest eggs you can find and peel them. Arrange them on a bed of salt and shake over a few drops of Tabasco sauce. They will look like a plateful of eyeballs!

Serve BAT sandwiches—with a filling of Bacon, Avocado, and Tomato!

For a novel party invitation, paint the party details on a large pumpkin and take a photograph. Have copies made and send them out to your guests.

Make toenail canapés by placing tortilla chips on a triangle of black pumpernickel and topping with a dollop of guacamole (gruesomely green), tomato salsa (gorily red), or brined pickle (sludgy brown).

What better drink to serve to grown-ups at Halloween than a Bloody Mary? For a generous jugful, mix 1 cup (250 ml) of vodka with 2 cups (500 ml) tomato juice, a generous squeeze of lemon, a pinch of celery salt and pepper, and Worcestershire and Tabasco sauce to taste. Add plenty of ice and a celery rib for stirring.

What's a ghoul's favorite fizzy drink?
—Lemon and slime.

Another gory-looking (but deliciously refreshing) alcoholic cocktail is a Strawberry Daiquiri. Place 24 strawberries and plenty of ice in a blender, pour in half a bottle of white rum, and blend for about 10 seconds. Pour into cocktail glasses and serve with straws.

Serve an Eyeball Highball to adult guests—gin and tonic served in tall glasses with pimento-stuffed olives frozen in ice cubes—these will look like frozen eyeballs when dropped into your guests' drinks.

Brew a batch of spiced ale—a traditional Halloween drink.

Pour 5 cups (1.2 liters) real English ale into a saucepan and add a pinch each of ground cloves, ground ginger, allspice, and a cinnamon stick. Bring almost to boiling point, stir in a glass of brandy and 1 tablespoon brown sugar. Serve immediately.

Behave badly at
the dinner table.
Slurp your soup
and blow
bubbles in your
drink through a
plastic straw.

Why do witches get stiff joints?
—They suffer from broomatism.

To create the right atmosphere in your house, replace the light bulbs with colored bulbs (available at your local hardware store). Black, red, blue, and green light bulbs cast an eerie glow.

On Halloween, witches are supposed to gather together for a party hosted by the devil. What a great theme! Throw a "witches and warlocks" party, and get all of your witchy party guests to turn up on broomsticks!

Have a grown-up pirate party. Pirate costumes are easy for most people to make—men can combine frilled shirts, striped T-shirts, spotted scarves, vests, short pants, and long leather boots, while women might prefer long skirts, petticoats, and tight bodices. Food can be served on metal plates and wooden boards, drinks served in goblets, and the decorations can include treasure chests brimming with coins and jewels, palm trees, and parrots.

To make Pirate Punch, mix a bottle of dark rum with the juice of 6 limes, a dash of Angostura bitters, and a grating of nutmeg. Fill glasses with ice, pour in the punch, and garnish with slices of lime.

Hide a cassette or CD player on the front porch to play scary Halloween sound effects or horror movie music as guests arrive.

For a haunted house party, guests can dress as ghosts, spooks, and specters. Drape old sheets over the furniture for a derelict and eerie feel.

Why didn't Dracula get married?
—He never met a nice enough ghoul.

Make use of fairy lights, which always create a wonderful effect. These days they are available in so many different shapes and sizes you'll have a hard time choosing. Use them indoors and outdoors— check that they are suitable for outdoor use—to create a marvelously magical mood for your Halloween party.

Another great party theme is "rock 'n' roll legends." Guests could dress as deceased rock stars such as Elvis Presley, Mama Cass, Janis Joplin, Bob Marley, Jim Morrison, or John Lennon.

Or have a colonial party, with your guests dressing in powdered wigs, opulent fabrics, tights, and buckled shoes.

Dress as a preacher. Wear a white shirt back to front, to create a "dog collar." A long black tunic or robe will add authenticity, and a pair of wire-rimmed glasses and a bible are good accessories.

Play some crazy Halloween music. What about "The Monster Mash," from way back in 1962, by Bobby Picket?

What do you call a witch with one leg?
—Eileen.

For a stylish dinner party, lay a number of small tables instead of one large one and place a crystal ball on each table as a centerpiece. Make a white "tombstone" place card for each place setting.

Serve roasted and salted pumpkin seeds with drinks. (See recipe on p210.)

What do you get when you drop a pumpkin?
—Squash.

What is the ratio of a pumpkin's circumference to its diameter?
—Pumpkin Pi.

Serve canapés on a Ouija board.

Hire an astrologer or tarot card reader for entertainment.

Clear out your fireplace and fill it with orange and black pillar candles in various shapes and sizes.

Make spiced cider punch for party guests by pouring 4 cups (1 liter) cider into a saucepan and adding 2 cinnamon sticks, a few cloves, 1 teaspoon allspice, 2 tablespoons brown sugar, and the juice of an orange. Heat to the simmering point. Place an orange slice and a cinnamon stick in each serving glass and ladle in the punch carefully.

Ladle punch from a traditional black cauldron, setting the cauldron in front of a tray of dry ice to give it atmosphere.

When purchasing dry ice, read all instructions and warnings. Keep dry ice away from children!

Get all the women at the party to stand behind a curtain with just their feet poking out. The men have to try to identify the women by their shoes. Swap places and get the men to stick out their feet. They may all agree to take off their socks and shoes, which makes the game even more fun!

A variation of the feet game is to get all the men to roll up their trousers. The women then take turns being blindfolded and try to identify the men by feeling their legs.

Hold a pumpkin carving competition. Ask everyone to bring a carved pumpkin to the party and set aside a place to display them. Let guests vote for their favorites and give a prize to the winner.

Make your own Halloween party soundtrack, with songs such as Michael Jackson's "Thriller," "Werewolves of London," "Bad Moon Rising," and "The Monster Mash."

Why not watch some scary movies? Choose from *The Witches of Eastwick*, *Halloween*, *Friday the Thirteenth*, or *An American Werewolf in London*.

Go and see a play with a spooky theme—like *Blithe Spirit* by Noël Coward—or why not try and get your hands on a script, gather a few friends together, and put on your own performance?

Play pass the bottle. Divide party guests into two teams and give each team an empty bottle. The object of the game is to pass the bottle from one team member to another, along the line, clasped between the knees.

Why was the witch doing magic, flat on her back? —Because the doctor had told her to lie down for a spell.

Murder in the dark is always fun. Decide who should be the murderer by getting each person to take a playing card. The person who takes the ace of spades is the murderer—but no one should reveal what card they have taken. Players should spread out around the house and when the murderer strikes, the victim should wait 5 seconds before screaming and falling to the floor. Nominate one person to be the detective and see if he or she can guess "whodunit."

NEWSPAPER FANCY DRESS. Split into teams and supply each team with some newspapers and pins or sticky tape. Team members must create newspaper costumes. The most creative wins a prize.

Wear a mask. It's a great disguise, and it's quicker and cheaper than makeup.

What brand of clothing do zombies wear?
—Decay NY!

With clever application of makeup, you can make yourself look like you've been in a fight. Smudge red and blue makeup around one eye and your cheekbone, to look like a bruise. Purchase fake blood from a party shop and apply it to your nostrils so it drips out. Push some cotton wool balls inside your mouth, between your teeth and top lip, so you look like you've been punched in the mouth. Buy some black tooth enamel and paint one or two of your teeth.

Be the most glamorous witch at the party! Wear false eyelashes, red lipstick, and talon-like red nails. Put on a glamorous, tightly-fitting, figure-enhancing black dress and cast your wicked spell.

Did you hear about Cinderella mouse?
—She saw a bat and thought it was her fairy godmother.

At home, dress up in sexy, vampish underwear, including stockings and high-heeled shoes. Behave disgracefully!

What did the vampire's wife say to her husband as he went off to work? —"Have a nice bite!"

Make up your bed with black satin sheets.

What's it like to be kissed by a vampire? —It's a pain in the neck.

When trick-or-treaters knock on your door, be a party pooper. Leave a sign on your front door telling all trick-or-treaters to "beware!" and brace yourself for the tricks they will play.

Give away something other than candy—something less attractive, such as a golf ball, a bag of sand, or a toilet roll. Watch those trick-or-treaters' faces fall!

What do little birds say on Halloween?
—"Twick-or-Tweet."

Wait behind the door and as soon as they arrive, jump out wearing a costume and holding a bag, yelling "trick-or-treat!"

"Knock, Knock."
"Who's there?"
"Boo!"
"Boo who?"
—"Don't cry, it's only me!"

Fill an old briefcase or handbag with scrap paper or old magazines and brochures. Write the words "Top Secret" on it in big letters and when trick-or-treaters knock on your door, act nervous, hand them the bag, and quickly shut the door.

Pretend that you think any trick-or-treaters are plumbers who have come to fix your pipes. Ask them what they think is wrong with your hot water heater and ask them how much it will cost to fix.

When you answer the door, act as though you are really scared by them and start running round in circles, screaming.

Why are there fences around cemeteries?
—Because people are dying to get in.

Before you part with any treats, tell them you expect each of them to do 20 push-ups.

Hand out a list of treats on offer, as if it were a restaurant menu, and ask them to choose. Ask them if they would like to see the wine list, too. Give them the treats and present them with a bill for what they have chosen.

Give away colored eggs. Say you're confused, you thought it was Easter and that they are dressed up as the Easter Bunny.

What happened to the man who didn't pay his exorcist bill? —He was repossessed.

Have a horrible Halloween!

History
and
Legend

The holiday we know as Halloween is a time when we celebrate all kinds of things—witchcraft, the harvest, and the spirits of the dead. But what are the origins of Halloween? You will discover that it has had many influences from many cultures over the centuries.

The Celts, who lived hundreds of years ago in what is now Great Britain and Northern France, worshipped nature and had many gods. They held festivals for two major gods—a sun god and a god of the dead, called Samhain—pronounced "sow-en."

The Celtic New Year was November 1 and marked the end of the season of the sun and the beginning of the season of darkness and cold,

The sun god was the favorite god of the Celts. He made the earth beautiful and was responsible for the crops in the fields.

According to Celtic legend, Samhain controlled the spirits of the dead and could allow them to rest peacefully or make them go wild on the night of October 31.

Which ghosts haunt skyscrapers? —High spirits.

On October 31, after the crops were harvested and stored for the long winter, cooking fires in the houses would be extinguished. The Druids—Celtic priests—would meet on hilltops in the dark oak forest, because oak trees were sacred and they would light new fires and offer sacrifices of crops and animals. As they danced around the fires, the season of the sun passed and the season of darkness would begin.

When the morning arrived, the Druids would give an ember from their fires to a member of each family. These people would then take the embers home to start new cooking fires. These fires would keep the homes warm and free from evil spirits.

The festival on November 1 for Samhain would last for three days. People would parade in costumes made from the skins and heads of animals. Dressing up is one of the customs that has been passed down through the centuries and is still incorporated into present-day Halloween rituals.

A stag—considered to be a symbol of royalty—would often be slaughtered as a sacrifice at Samhain.

During the first century, the Romans invaded Britain and brought with them many of their festivals and customs. One of these was Pomona Day, also celebrated around November 1 and named after their goddess of fruits and gardens.

In AD 835, the Roman Catholic Church made November 1 a church holiday to honor all the saints and called it All Saints' Day—otherwise known as Hallowmas, or All Hallows.

In old English, the word "hallow" meant "sanctify." Roman Catholics, Episcopalians, and Lutherans used to observe All Hallows' Day to honor all Saints in heaven, known or unknown. They used to consider it one of the most significant observances of the Church year. Catholics were obliged to attend Mass.

What fairytale do ghosts like best? —Sleeping Boo-ty.

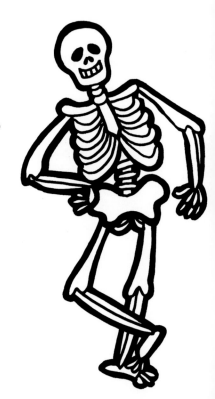

In Scotland, the Cailleach Bheur or blue-faced hag, who personified winter, was reborn every year at Halloween. She was said to creep over the land, killing off the last of the crops with her magic stick. Scottish farmers would leave the last sheaf of corn uncut in the field. Then, at Halloween—or Samhain—it would be cut and dressed as an old woman with an apron. Bread and cheese would be put in the pockets of the apron and the "auld wife" would be carried back to the farm to preside over the feast.

Years later, the Church decided to make November 2 a holy day, too. It was called All Souls' Day and was a time to honor the dead. It was celebrated with big bonfires, parades, and people dressing up as saints, angels, and devils.

Over the centuries, the customs from all these holidays—Samhain, Pomona Day, All Saints, and All Souls, became combined until eventually October 31 became known as All Hallows' Eve, and later, Halloween.

The influences on Halloween from Pomona Day are apples, nuts, and harvest rituals, while the Festival of Samhain gives us black cats, magic, evil spirits, and death. All Saints' Day and All Souls' Day give us spirits, ghosts, skeletons, and skulls.

Spiritual festivals at this time of the year are not an exclusively Celtic, Roman, or Christian tradition—cultures all over the world have rituals and festivals at the end of October and the beginning of November.

The Romans observed the holiday of Feralia, intended to give rest and peace to the departed, on February 21, the end of the Roman year. In the seventh century, Pope Boniface IV introduced All Saints' Day to replace the pagan festival of the dead and it was observed on May 13. Later, Pope Gregory III changed the date to November 1. The Greek Orthodox Church observes it on the first Sunday after Pentecost.

Indians celebrate Divali, a Hindu holiday on November 2. Just like the Irish custom of keeping candles in the window at Halloween, the traditional way to mark Divali is to light candles and kerosene oil lamps.

In Austria, and in the German region of Bavaria, the period between October 30 and November 8 is designated as *Seleenwoche*, or All Souls' Week.

In Mexico, Halloween is celebrated as *Los Días de Los Muertos*—the Days of the Dead. Families have picnics in cemeteries, decorating relatives' graves with flowers and ribbons.

In Wales, Halloween is known as *Nos Galen-gaeof*— the Night of the Winter Calends.

The word "bonfire," originally "boon-fire," means a huge fire built to honor the spirits of the air, to invoke favors, and to drive off evil spirits.

The first full moon between winter solstice and Halloween is called the harvest moon, the hunter's moon, or the blood moon.

What kind of mistakes do ghosts make?
—Boo boos.

The tradition of bobbing for apples may have its origins with Pomona day. The apple also has strong associations with Demeter, the Roman goddess of harvest and agriculture. Bobbing for apples is considered by some to be a fertility rite, or a way of forecasting who you will marry.

Houdini, the famous escapologist and magician, died on Halloween, 1926, of a ruptured appendix, after having been punched in the stomach by a university student.

There is an old Irish legend about a drunk called Jack. Out in the woods one day, he tricked Satan into climbing a tree to throw down some fruit. Jack carved a cross into the tree, trapped the devil and struck a bargain so that Satan  would leave his soul alone when he died. But when Jack died, heaven would not take him either. He pestered the devil to let him in, but Satan gave him a burning ember instead. He carried the ember in a hollowed-out turnip to light his way as he wandered through eternal darkness on earth. Eventually this was replaced with the pumpkin in North America and became the modern jack-o'-lantern.

In Finland, people had their own version of "Jack"—the soul of a child buried in the forest.

In many places, folklore tells of a will-o'-the-wisp who wanders about swamp areas, enticing victims to follow, lighting fires called "foolish fire" because only a fool would follow them.

In the late nineteenth century the Irish believed that the "little people," or fairies, played pranks on Halloween.

What did one ghost say to the other ghost? —"Do you believe in people?"

On the last Thursday in October, Somerset folk celebrated Punkie Night. It is said to have started in a town called Hinton St. George, when a group of men got drunk at a local fair and couldn't find their way home. The women went out to find their husbands, carrying lanterns made from hollowed-out mangel-worzels, a kind of rutabaga or turnip, known as "punkies." In subsequent years, children would parade through villages carrying punkie lanterns and singing a special song.

A ghost went to see the doctor and said, "Doctor, doctor, people can't see me."
—The doctor called out, "Next, please!"

What does a vampire fear most?

In Celtic times, disguise was a form of protection. By dressing up as ghosts, the living could blend in with the dead and lead a parade to lure the real spirits away from villages.

In Europe, during medieval times and later, elves, fairies, and witches—who occasionally took the shape of cats—were believed to fly on All Hallows' Eve, and bonfires were lit to ward off these spirits. Vestiges of these beliefs and practices persisted in Scotland and Ireland for centuries.

Halloween was also a time for games and rituals involving methods of foretelling the future. Young people indulged in certain rituals to try to determine their marital prospects.

There was an old Irish country practice of going from door to door, collecting money, bread, cakes, nuts, and apples in preparation for the festival of St. Columbus Kill.

**Who is the emperor of the French skeletons?
—Napoleon Boneaparte.**

Another Irish custom was begging for soul cakes in exchange for blessings and promises of prosperity or protection against bad luck.

Since the Irish believed that fairies were abroad on the night of Halloween, many people would leave an offering of food or milk on the steps of their house so the occupants would be blessed by the "good folk" for the coming year.

Food was also left on Irish doorsteps for people who had died.

The Irish and the Scots had their "night of mischief" when boys would assemble in gangs and visit neighborhood houses. They would cause a great disturbance and the householders would be expected to bribe them with treats to make them go away.

In nineteenth-century America, rural immigrants from Ireland and Scotland carried on their customs. Girls would stay indoors, performing rituals to forecast their marriage prospects, while boys went out and engaged in pranks. Meanwhile, the elders would blame all the mayhem on the fact that the spirits were abroad that night.

Who do monsters go to for psychiatric treatment?
—Shrinkenstein.

In mid-nineteenth-century New York, children called "ragamuffins" would dress in costumes and beg for pennies from adults on Thanksgiving Day. In the 1930s, the Depression made this begging more real and some of the tricks more menacing. Towns and cities began to organize "safe" Halloween events and householders would hand out bribes to the neighborhood children. The ragamuffins either stopped their Thanksgiving begging or started doing it on Halloween instead.

Hey, hey for Halloween!
Then the witches shall be seen,
Some in black and some in green,
Hey, hey for Halloween!

(Traditional rhyme)

The name witch comes from the Saxon term *wica*, meaning "wise one."

Witches have been connected with Halloween for centuries. Legends tell of witches gathering twice a year when the seasons changed, on the eve of May Day (April 30) and on All Hallows' Eve (October 31).

Witches would gather on these nights, arriving on broomsticks, to celebrate at a party hosted by the devil. Superstitious rumors told of witches casting spells on unsuspecting people, transforming themselves into different forms, and causing other magical mischief.

How do you picture yourself
flying on a broom?
—By witchful thinking.

Three of the most famous witches appear in Shakespeare's *Macbeth*—and they can foretell the future. They brew up a potion in a cauldron, adding all kinds of strange ingredients:

**"Eye of newt, toe of frog,
Wool of bat and tongue of dog,
Adder's fork and blind worm's sting,
Lizard's leg and howlet's wing."**

A witch's familiar is something—usually an animal—that amplifies a witch's power and protects her from negative forces. When the early settlers went to North America, they took their belief in witches with them. Legends of witches spread and mixed with the beliefs of Native Americans, who also believed in witches, and later with the beliefs of the African slaves.

The black cat is a popular symbol of Halloween, probably because the Celts believed that black cats were people who had been changed into animals because of evil magic.

Much of the common perception of witches today goes back to images created by the church and civil courts to create hysteria and fear. The church tried to eradicate the influence of witches by persecution, torture, and murder. But it was likely that many of the "witches" that lost their lives were only midwives.

To "prove" whether or not someone was a witch, the victim was ducked under water. If she floated, she was called a witch. If she drowned, she was innocent—but either way, she died.

It is estimated that between the fifteenth and eighteenth centuries, approximately two million people were executed for witchcraft and 80 percent of them were women.

What do you call a witch's garage? —A broom closet.

The last person to be executed in Europe for being a witch was Anna Goddi, who was hanged in Switzerland in 1782.

The name "warlock," to describe a male version of a witch, is a derivation of the Saxon word "war-loek," meaning oath-breaker.

The Irish writer Bram (Abraham) Stoker made up the character for his novel, *Dracula*, over a hundred years ago. In the story, Dracula is tall and thin with red eyes, pale skin, and pointed fangs. He can change into a bat or a wolf and also disappear in an evil mist.

Why did Dracula take a spoonful of medicine? —To stop his coffin.

The character of Count Dracula may actually be based on a cruel prince, Vlad Dracula, who ruled in Transylvania 500 years ago and was known for killing his enemies by driving a sharp stake through their bodies.

Where did the vampire open his savings account?
—At a blood bank.

Dracula's castle may also be based on a real castle—Bran Castle in Transylvania—which still remains very popular with tourists to this day.

People from Transylvania were afraid of vampires and believed that a corpse would become a vampire if a cat jumped over it before it was buried.

They also thought you would become a vampire if you were born with teeth!

A vampire is a corpse that comes to life at night to drink people's blood while they sleep.

Which building does Dracula visit in New York?
—The Vampire State Building.

In Central and South America, there are real vampire bats with sharp teeth. They drink the blood of horses, cattle, and other animals.

Why does Dracula keep shouting at everyone?
—Because he has a bat temper.

The story of Frankenstein was written in 1818 by English writer, Mary Shelley, who thought it up for a ghost-story competition. In the story, Dr Victor Frankenstein builds a man using dead body parts taken from graveyards. He is brought to life with a flash of lightning—but people are frightened by his appearance and he ends up as a murderous monster.

What did Frankenstein say when he was struck by lightning?
—"Great! That was just what I needed."

At the time when Mary Shelley wrote her novel, scientists sometimes took bodies from graves to dissect and study. Mary Shelley hoped her story would warn of the dangers of experiments on human beings and that it would teach people not to treat others badly just because of their appearance.

Frankenstein was the subject of one of the first horror films. Made in 1931, the film starred the actor Boris Karloff as the monster.

What do you call a clever monster?
—Frank Einstein.

The tomb of the boy-king Tutankhamun lay undisturbed in the Valley of the Kings for over 3,200 years until English archaeologist Howard Carter discovered it in 1922. But it was said that the dead pharaoh had laid a curse on anyone who entered the tomb—and, sure enough, Carter's friend, Lord Caernarfon, died only four months later.

What kind of streets do zombies walk down?
—Dead ends.

Death shall come on swift wings to whoever touches the tomb of the Pharaoh.
(Inscription on Tutankhamun's tomb)

The Mummy, a horror movie made in 1932, was inspired by the curse of Tutankhamun. Boris Karloff played the part of the mummy.

To mummify a body, all the organs except the heart were removed, the body was dried with salt, which took about 40 days, and was then treated with spices, wine, and resin (the sticky part of the sap in some trees). Finally, the body was stuffed with linen and sand and wrapped in bandages. The organs were preserved separately in jars, ready for use in the afterlife.

Many objects—such as a fan, jewelry, clothes, food, and furniture—were left in a mummy's tomb to help it on its journey to the afterlife. Scenes from the ancient Egyptian *Book of the Dead* were often painted on the mummy case or tomb walls.

Mythical werewolves are said to have magical powers—the main one being the ability to transform themselves into wolves. They are evil creatures that live off the flesh of human beings.

Real wolves do not usually attack human beings, although there are tales of mysterious wolf-like beasts that have done so.

The werewolf legend may have arisen out of a rare disease called porphyria. The symptoms included excessive hair growth, a pulling back of the muscles of the face to reveal more of the teeth, and sensitivity to sunlight.

What's a monster's favorite Shakespeare play?
—Romeo and Ghouliet.

How does a man become a werewolf? Some say that if you drink water from a puddle in a wolf's footprint you will become a werewolf. Others say that if you are bitten by a werewolf you will become one, too. Legend has it that a man may also be born a werewolf.

A belief in alien life has been around for thousands of years—even the ancient Greeks and Romans recorded sightings of peculiar, unexplained objects in the sky. Today we call these sightings UFOs (Unidentified Flying Objects) and some people believe that UFOs are alien spacecraft.

What do you say to a ghost with three heads? —"Hello, hello, hello."

There were so many reports of sightings of different types of spacecraft in the USA in the 1960s that the US Air Force paid scientists to carry out a special study. Most UFOs were found to be natural phenomena, such as meteors, planets, or stars, and some turned out to be ordinary aircraft.

When does a skeleton laugh? —When something tickles his funny bone.

Skeletons, of course, represent the dead, reminding us that Halloween is a celebration of life and death.

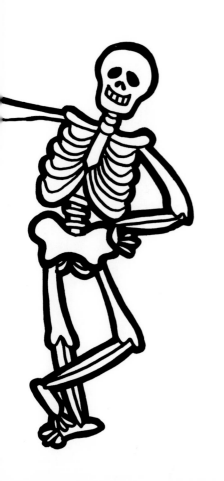

Why aren't there any famous skeletons? —They're a bunch of no-bodies!

A ghoul is supposedly an evil spirit who robbed graves to eat the dead. Nineteenth-century grave robbers who provided doctors with fresh corpses on which to experiment were also called ghouls.

What do you call a skeleton who refuses to help around the house? —Lazybones.

Goblins are ugly, mischievous sprites, sometimes called hobgoblins.

A banshee is a supernatural creature, an ancestral spirit who appears to warn Irish people of their time of death. According to tradition, the banshee only visits five major Irish families: the O'Neills, the O'Briens, the O'Connors, the O'Gradys, and the Kavanaghs.

**What do you call a troll with a broken leg?
—A hoblin goblin.**

According to legend, a banshee will appear in one of three guises: as a young woman, a middle-aged matron, or an old ugly woman or hag.
She sometimes dresses as a washerwoman, washing the bloody clothes of those who are going to die. Some people believe she appears in a variety of animal forms associated with witchcraft, such as a hooded crow, an ermine (or stoat), a hare, or a weasel.

What was the ghost doing at the station?
—Waiting for a ghost train.

Trolls originate in Scandinavia. Some are large and evil, while others are small and play tricks on people.

The most terrifying aspect of the banshee is her screeching wail, heard mostly at night when someone is about to die.

Customs
and
Superstitions

From ghoulies and ghosties
   and long-leggedy beasties
And things that go bump
   in the night,
Good Lord, deliver us.

                    (Cornish prayer)

Halloween has, for centuries, been a time for
games and rituals. Most of the customs that have
been observed through the ages are remnants of
ancient religious beliefs. We think we live in a
sophisticated age, but even today many customs
and superstitions linger on.

Do you believe in magic? Then Halloween is the night for you.

October is the time for celebrating the year's harvest and for performing certain rituals and following certain customs to make sure that next year's harvest will also be good.

Who writes letters
to Dracula?
—Members of his fang club.

All over Britain, great ceremony was attached to harvesting the last sheaf of corn. It would be made into a corn doll, created by braiding the stalks together and this would be kept until the spring. People believed that the corn spirit lived in the husks and as the crop of wheat, barley, or rye was harvested, the spirit fled to the last few stalks which remained. By creating the corn doll the spirit would be kept alive for the next year and the new crop.

Corn dolls were hung in the barn, the farmhouse, and sometimes the local church. In spring, farmers plowed them back into the soil.

In Christian churches all over Britain, and in some schools, services are still held to thank God for the harvest and to pray for a good harvest next year. Local people or schoolchildren bring baskets of fruit and vegetables to decorate the church and this produce is then distributed among the poor or the elderly.

At Halloween the wind at midnight is supposed to indicate the prevailing wind for the coming season. And if there is a moon on Halloween, it is an omen—a clear moon means fine weather.

Clouds racing across the face
of the moon on Halloween
mean storms are on the way.

Throw a stone into the fire. The next day, when the fire is out and the ashes are cold, retrieve your stone and you will be assured of good fortune for the coming year. If you cannot find your stone in the ashes, it means bad luck.

Throw nuts on the fire to determine your fortune for the year ahead. The way each one burns has a special meaning. If a nut burns brightly, you will have good health. If it flares up with a sudden bright light, you will get married!

Throw two nuts on a fire. Give each the names of a potential lover. The one that cracks first is the one for you!

Hazelnuts were named after an individual and thrown into the bonfire on the eve of Samhain (the Celtic name for Halloween). The way the nut burned was thought to determine that person's fate for the coming year.

The hazelnut was sacred to ancient Celts, who believed that the nuts had divining powers. They also believed that these powers were especially powerful on Halloween, so, they frequently used them in marriage divinations.

Why not visit a cemetery or a haunted house at Halloween—if you dare!

Apple-bobbing is another ancient custom. Float apples in a tub of water, which represents the cauldron of rebirth, and try to catch one using only your teeth.

Peel an apple in one long continuous strip and allow the peel to fall on the floor. It will form the initials of your future husband or wife.

What is a vampire's favorite mode of transportation? —A blood vessel.

Eat an apple while looking in a mirror and you'll see the face of your future husband looking over your shoulder.

If you hold a mirror on Halloween and walk backwards down the stairs, the face that appears in the mirror will be your next lover.

Lean backward and look down a well. You will see your future reflected in the water below.

Sweep around the base of a corn stack with a broom three times. Third time around, your future marriage partner is supposed to appear.

Once upon a time, girls were sent out blindfolded, in pairs, to pull the first cabbages from the field. If there was a lot of earth attached to the root, it was believed that they would have plenty of money—but if there was only a little earth, they would be poor.

How did the skeleton know it was going to rain?
—He could feel it in his bones!

Why can't skeletons play music in church?
—Because they have no organs.

The taste of the first cabbage pulled from the field is supposed to reveal something about a girl's future husband—will he be sweet or bitter?

In Somerset, if you cracked an egg and discovered it had a double yolk, it was supposed to mean there would be a hurried wedding due to a pregnancy.

If you stumble as you are going upstairs, it foretells a wedding.

When a newly married couple reach their new home, tradition states that the bride should be carried over the threshold by her new husband. This is to avoid the evil spirits that gather there.

**Why was the mummy so tense?
—He was all wound up.**

Carrying a baby three times around the house will protect it from colic.

If you live in North Yorkshire, you will know that it is the custom to place a silver coin in a baby's hand when you are visiting for the first time.

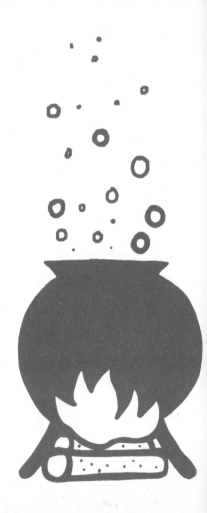

Bake a pudding—the traditional choice was a kind of porridge or "crowdie," made from oatmeal with cream, sugar, and rum—and hide some traditional charms inside. Each person around the table takes a spoonful in turn until they unearth one of the following charms:

A coin for wealth
A ring for marriage
A button for a bachelor
A thimble for a spinster
A wishbone for your heart's desire.

In Ireland, 100 years ago or so, young men carried out practical jokes that required a great degree of physical strength. They might, for example, overturn a small building or place a cart on the roof.

On November 2, All Souls' Day, carry on an ancient custom by dressing up as a saint, an angel, or a devil.

On Irish farms, some families would sprinkle holy water on animals at Halloween.

Why did the game warden arrest the ghost?
—Because he didn't have a haunting license.

Place a lighted candle on the floor and jump over it. If the flame goes out, you will have bad luck for the coming year.

Jack be nimble, Jack be quick
Jack jump over the candlestick.

(Traditional rhyme)

What do you call a ghoul who gets too close to a bonfire?
—A toasty ghosty.

It has long been a tradition in Ireland to light a candle for each deceased relative in the room where the death occurred.

In Latin countries, people put candles in churchyards and cemeteries.

Burn an effigy of a witch on a Halloween bonfire. This was a popular nineteenth-century tradition. The dummy would be wheeled through the village in a handcart before being tossed onto the fire.

It's Punkie Night tonight!
It's Punkie Night tonight!
Give us a candle, give us a light.
If you don't, you'll get a fright!

(Traditional rhyme)

According to Irish folklore, a plain wooden cross was placed on the thatched roof of a cottage, or just inside the front door, to ward off evil spirits.

If an animal on an Irish farm showed signs of illness on October 31, people would spit on it to banish evil spirits.

**What does a headless horseman never suffer from?
—A headache.**

If a farm animal died on an Irish farm at Halloween, holy water would be scattered in the place for years to follow.

Be careful not to break a mirror or you will have seven years of bad luck.

For over 300 years, hollow glass spheres, called witches' balls, have been hung in windows to ward off witch's spells. You sometimes see them hanging up in antique stores or used as garden decorations.

Where does a ghost go on vacation?
—Mali-boo.

Follow the Irish custom of keeping candles lit in your windows at Halloween.

In Pendle, Lancashire, people would gather at the Malkin Tower for the ceremony of Lighting the Witches! A brave soul would walk around the tower clockwise, carrying a lit candle. If the flame flickered or died, bad luck would follow—but if it stayed alight, evil spirits would be banished.

If a candle flame suddenly turns blue, it means there's a ghost nearby.

The celtic term "Samhain" means "summer's end" and was used to describe the night when the dead were believed to reappear. The following day—November 1— was the first day of winter, so Samhain is the turning point between the old year and the new.

Samhain is traditionally the time for settling debts, for workmen to be paid their wages, and for rents to be paid. So follow this custom and settle your debts!

Beware! Halloween is the time when mortals are most likely to be abducted by hobgoblins, evil spirits, and fairies.

If you do meet a fairy on Halloween, throw the dust from under your feet at them. This obliges them to surrender any mortals they are keeping captive.

If you are traveling at Halloween, carry a black-handled knife or a steel needle, for protection against evil spirits.

How does Frankenstein sit in his chair? —Bolt upright.

**Heigh ho for Halloween
When the fairies a' are seen,
Some black and some green.
Heigh ho for Halloween!**
(Traditional rhyme)

Anyone disposing of water at Halloween should call out "seachain" as a warning to fairies to get out of the way.

Do not eat decaying fruits in November—the "puca"—the Celtic name for the "little people" or fairies—spit or urinate on them. (A timely warning, in order to discourage youngsters from getting a tummyache.)

Country housewives once believed that food would be spoilt if it was stirred "widdershins"—in the opposite direction to the east-west movement of the sun.

Do zombies like being dead?
—Of corpse they do!

A watched pot never boils.

In Dorset, people believed that a slow-boiling kettle was bewitched and might even contain a toad!

In Yorkshire, housewives believed that bread would not rise if there was a corpse anywhere nearby.

Yorkshire folk also believed that if you cut both ends off a loaf of bread, the devil would fly over the house.

Where do most American werewolves live?
—Howly-wood, California.

Never seat 13 people at the table for your Halloween meal—it will bring bad luck.

How do ghosts begin their letters?
—Tomb it may concern…

Where do ghosts mail their letters?
—At the ghost office.

If someone spills the salt, they must throw a pinch over their left shoulder, into the eyes of the devil.

If you find crossed knives on the table, it is supposed to signify that there will be a quarrel.

If you have a white tablecloth on your table, do not leave it on overnight because that would mean that the household will need a shroud in the near future.

Two women are not supposed to pour from the same teapot. If they do, a quarrel will ensue.

When you have finished eating a hard-cooked egg from its shell, push the spoon through the bottom of the empty shell to let the devil out.

In Ulster, fairies were believed to be fallen angels.

Oatmeal and salt were put on children's heads in Northern Ireland to protect them.

In Europe, during medieval times and later, bonfires were lit to ward off spirits such as elves, fairies, and witches. Light a bonfire this Halloween. It's also a great way to keep warm on a chilly evening.

In Scotland and Ireland, Halloween was called the "night of mischief." So get up to some mischief of your own this Halloween!

In Ireland and Scotland, villagers once lit bonfires either to guide the spirits of the dead back to their homes or to drive them away.

Telling ghost stories is just the thing to do on Halloween. Get some friends together and let everyone tell a few.

The Irish love a good ghost story. Irishman James Joyce wrote about a black dog with eyes like carriage lamps and Oscar Wilde wrote about the paranormal.

Dress all in black, like a witch, to be like the night.

How does a silly witch know
what time it is?
—She looks at her witch-watch.

**The cone shape of the witch's hat
was believed to direct energy from
higher dimensions to her mind and
down through her body.**

Witches carry lanterns to illuminate the world above and below.

The witch's broom is made from male and female components, to symbolize the joining together of a man and woman, or god and goddess. The male part of the broom is the shaft—usually made from ash—and the female part, the twigs, made from willow or birch.

Have your own Halloween party this year. Dress up as the devil and ask all your guests to dress as witches!

How do monsters fly?
—In a scare-o-plane.

It was believed that witches flew on broomsticks because the broom symbolized the link between home life and travel to other spiritual dimensions.

Superstition tells of witches casting spells on unsuspecting people, transforming them into different forms. Would you like to be a frog?

If you want to meet a witch, put your clothes on inside out and walk backwards on Halloween night.

The black cat has been associated with witches for a long time and many superstitions have evolved about cats. It was believed that witches could change into cats. Some people also believed that cats were the spirits of the dead.

In some parts of the United Kingdom, seeing two or three ravens together is considered bad luck.

Some people also believe it is unlucky to see only one magpie but different numbers seen together bring different kinds of fortune, as told in the traditional rhyme:

One for sorrow,
Two for joy,
Three for a girl,
Four for a boy,
Five for silver,
Six for gold,
Seven for a secret never to be told.

Why did the Cyclops have to close down his school?
—He only had one pupil.

Why not follow the old Irish peasant practice of going from door to door, collecting money, bread, cake, cheese, eggs, butter, nuts, apples, and other items in preparation for the festival of St. Columbus Kill?

A piece of red thread is believed by some to be a cure for hiccups—just tie it around your finger and they will stop.

Tie a piece of red thread around the branch of a tree to ward off witches. It is particularly effective if the branch is from a Rowan tree.

Rowan tree and red thread make The witches tine their speed.

(Scottish rhyme)

Poor people used to offer their richer neighbors prayers for departed relatives in return for soul cakes (you will find a recipe for soul cakes on p170).

Or they would beg neighbors for soul cakes in exchange for promises of prosperity or protection against bad luck. If the residents of the houses you visit refuse to supply you with soul cakes—or other treats, for that matter—you were expected to play a practical joke on them. Sound familiar…?

Soul cakes were not the only things a poor neighbor would be pleased to accept. Fruit, sweets, or money would also be most welcome!

A soul, a soul, a soul cake,
Please, good missus, a soul cake,
An apple, a pear, plum, or a cherry,
Or any good thing to make us merry.

(Traditional rhyme)

The traditional drink to accompany soul cakes is spiced ale (for a recipe, turn to p327).

Before you eat a soul cake, say these traditional words:
"A soul cake, a soul cake,
Have mercy, Lord, on all
Christian souls."

In Scotland, trick-or-treating was known as "guising." Children would dress up or disguise themselves and visit houses, performing party pieces. Why not perform your own party piece— a song, dance, or poem—instead of playing tricks this Halloween?

Leave an offering of food or milk on the steps of your house for the fairies, and you will receive blessings for the year ahead.

Or maybe you would prefer to leave a meal or "dumb supper" on your steps for the spirits of the departed?

A "dumb supper" is also the name given to the custom of setting extra places at a dinner table, for the dead.

Eat your own evening meal in silence on Halloween, in honor of those who can no longer speak.

How do monsters tell their future?
—They read their horrorscope.

If you eat an apple without first rubbing it, you will be challenging the devil.

An old Lancashire custom involved picking up burning hay with a pitchfork and tossing it into the air, to scare away any witches that might be flying overhead.

The devil can transform himself into any animal—except a donkey.

On November 2, in some Irish houses, the poker and fire tongs were placed in the shape of a cross on the hearth.

If a man wants to know something about his future wife, he should pull up a cabbage from the ground. From the size of the stalk and the amount of earth clinging to it, he will know if she's going to be tall or short, fat or thin, rich or poor.

Leaving food on your doorstep is supposed to keep hungry spirits from entering your house.

Witchcraft is the use of special powers by one person to physically harm another—by casting a spell, chanting magic words or making gestures.

Witches were believed to turn themselves into hares. If a hunter shot such a hare it would not die but turn back into a witch—and the bullet wound would be visible. In order to kill a "witch hare," a hunter would have to use silver bullets.

Many people believed that hares were unlucky. If a pregnant woman encountered one, it was believed her baby would be born with a "hare lip."

To protect a house from witches, plant a mountain ash in the yard.

If someone enters your house on Halloween, make sure they leave by the same door. It is bad luck if they enter through the front door and leave through the back door, or vice versa.

If a number of people are sitting in a room and the door opens by itself, the person who closes it will be the first to die.

How many witches does it take to change a light bulb? —It depends what you want to change it into.

Under no circumstances must hawthorn be brought into the house before May Day because it belongs to the woodland god and will bring bad luck!

On Halloween the old ghosts come
About us—and they speak to some.

(Anonymous rhyme)

**People once thought that witches
had familiars—animal companions
that could carry out their wishes.
That's why, if a black cat crosses
your path, there is a chance it might
put a curse on you.**

Did you hear about the dog trainer who
joined a coven?
—He went from wags to witches.

The word "abracadabra" is supposed to be a powerful charm against certain ailments, including toothache.

The origin of the word "abracadabra" is unclear but many people believe it is a secret word, meaning "demon."

Potions—remarkable brews with unusual ingredients and amazing effects—have always been an essential part of the magician's tool-kit. The witches of classical mythology cooked up potions to restore youth, turn men into animals, and make themselves invisible. Medieval legends and fairytales tell of sleeping potions, love potions, potions of forgetfulness, and potions to cause jealousy and strife.

According to popular lore, witches usually left their homes via the chimney.

Between about 1450 and 1600, when belief in the power of witchcraft was widespread in Europe, witches were reported to take to the skies and head to their midnight gatherings astride not only broomsticks, but goats, oxen, sheep, dogs, and wolves, as well as shovels and staffs!

If a woman touches a Logan stone nine times at midnight, she will become a witch.

Witches can be prevented from flying off, or be brought down from the skies, by the peal of church bells. In the early seventeenth century, one German town was so fearful of witches that, for a time, churches would ring their bells continuously from dusk until dawn.

Scotland was the only place in Britain to burn witches to death. Even after this practice had ceased, children would run around the village, banging on people's doors, and asking them for peat for the fire, "to burn the witch."

What do you call a witch who lives at the beach?
—A sand-witch.

**What do you call two witches who live together?
—Broom-mates.**

In North America, it's bad luck if a black cat crosses your path—and good luck if a white cat does the same.

In Britain and Ireland, it's the opposite—a black cat spells good luck!

Some people believe that if a black cat crosses your path, you should turn around and go back or bad luck will strike you.

Witches, though most often associated with cats, had other animal companions, such as weasels, toads, and mice—and they were believed to nourish them with their own milk.

The buds of the willow branch are thought to resemble a cat's paws.

Some merry, friendly, country-folks
Together did convene,
To burn their nits, and pou their stocks,
An' haud their Hallowe'en.

(Robert Burns)

It was once believed that if a sparrow entered a house, it was an omen of death to the person who lived there. To avoid bad luck, the sparrow would be caught and killed to prevent the omen coming true.

In some places, black rabbits were thought to host the souls of human beings.

White rabbits are believed by some to be witches. Be sure to say "white rabbits" on November 1— and the first day of every month— to ensure good luck.

A rabbit's foot is a popular lucky charm.

Some people believe that a cat knows whether a dead person's spirit has gone to heaven, or not. Immediately after a death, if the cat of the house climbs a tree, the soul is bound for heaven; if the cat is already up a tree and climbs down, the soul is destined for hell.

If you ring a bell on Halloween, it will scare evil spirits away.

In Scotland, anyone who had to travel on Halloween night would carry a piece of rowan wood—a stick or a twig—to ward off witches. Even today, rowan wood is often used to make walking sticks.

If you see a spider on Halloween, it may well be the spirit of a dead loved one who is watching over you.

In the middle ages, it was believed that witches were closely associated with bats. If you see bats flying around and hear their cries, it means bad luck will come your way.

Before sunset on Halloween, walk around your home three times, backward and counter-clockwise, to ward off evil spirits.

**Why do ghosts go round scaring people?
—They're just trying to eek out a living.**

Wear black if you want to be wise. Native Americans associate black with learning and wisdom.

The moon was believed by to be a symbol of mysteries by Native Americans.

Gifts of food to the spirit world are supposed to ensure that next year's crop will be bountiful.

Organize a séance on Halloween. You might be more likely to make contact with spirits on this very special night.

Why couldn't the mummy answer the phone? —Because he was tied up!

The Egyptians believed that a mummy's heart was weighed by the gods before the person could gain eternal life. The heart was weighed against a feather, the Egyptian symbol of truth and, if the heart balanced with it, the mummy could pass safely into the afterlife. If the heart was too heavy, however, it was thrown away to be eaten by a monster.

Keep an eye on the church porch. It was once believed that if you watched the porch, or looked through the keyhole, you would discover who was to die in the coming year.

Listen at the church door on Halloween night and you will hear a ghostly voice speaking the names of those who will soon be buried in the cemetery.

This Halloween, set out a bowl of fruit or some other treat so that spirits (and small children dressed in costumes!) will leave you in peace.

Why is a ghost different from an owl?
—It frightens people but doesn't give a hoot.

Don't
go out—
there
are spirits
about!